Far, Far From Home:

The Ninth Florida Regiment in the Confederate Army

Gary Loderhose

Guild Press
Carmel, Indiana

ISBN# 1-57860-097-9

Library of Congress No. 99-71528

Guild Press Emmis Publishing, LP
10665 Andrade Drive
Zionsville, IN 46077
1-800-913-9563

To Lilla Curtis, who introduced me to the Hunters.

CONTENTS

INTRODUCTION

Christmas night, 1980, my mother-in-law presented me with a packet of old musty papers. To my surprise they were authentic Civil War letters once belonging to her stepfather Thompson Niblack. At that time I was attending Flagler College in St. Augustine majoring in history. She felt I could best utilize this treasure. Thus, I embarked upon an eighteen-year project that culminated with the publication of this book.

Far, Far From Home is the incredible story of an unsung American hero, his son, and the Confederate regiment in which they served. This book is about Florida as a new frontier state and the independent spirit of her soldiers facing overwhelming adversity. It is also the story of what the final year of the war was like for the average Confederate soldier serving in Virginia battling foes more threatening than the Yankees: disease, starvation, and anxiety over the welfare of families left behind, and real despair.

The book is footnoted for reference. Background Chapter One, "Antebellum Florida to Secession," is an exception, however. Research for Chapter One was drawn primarily from Charlton Tebeau's *A History of Florida* and Robert A. Taylor's *Rebel Storehouse: Florida in the Confederate Economy.* Quotations were taken from *Florida a Hundred Years Ago,* edited by Samuel Proctor.

I would like to thank those who helped with this project. Particular thanks are due my brother Rick who helped with the research in the early days and to close friend Bob Johns for his meticulous work on maps. Thanks to Lilla Curtis for giving me the Hunter letters and to Vercil and Ann Senseman of Fort Myers for allowing me to copy additional Hunter letters, as well as letters of Joseph Young. Appreciation is due to Dr. Thomas Graham, Professor of History, Flagler College, for reading the manuscript and offering insights on Florida's history. Special thanks go to my children, Emily, Benjamin, and William Addison, who lovingly put up with their exhausted father during the two month rewrite. I owe particular gratitude to my wife Karen, who is always encouraging me, supporting me, and cheerfully typing my work. Last, my respects to the memory of William Addison Hunter, whose faith in God endured throughout a horrible time in history, for setting an example, and for helping to strengthen my faith in the much less personally demanding times of today.

Gary Loderhose
Cape Coral, Florida
January 30, 1999

PREFACE

William Addison Hunter, one of the soldiers whose letters made possible this intimate telling of the Ninth Florida's history, was the grandson of an Irishman named Nathan Hunter. W. A.'s grandfather immigrated to America from County Antrim in Northern Ireland during the 1780s. He brought with him his wife Mary and five children: William, Joseph, Jane, Elizabeth, and James. Nathan settled a piece of land near a small village, which was curiously called Frog Level, located in the wild upcountry of South Carolina. According to legend Frog Level, later renamed Prosperity, received its strange name from a story about an old drunkard, a pond, and many frogs. The South Carolina upcountry was untamed land bordering on hostile Cherokee Indian Territory.

In the immediate years following their arrival, three additional children were born to Nathan and Mary: two sons, George and Nathan Jr., and a daughter, Mary. After establishing the family home, Nathan and his sons rooted themselves in the land, clearing, tilling, and cultivating it. There they prospered and gained respect throughout their community.

In 1808 Nathan and his sons traveled to nearby Newberry, the county seat, and were granted United States citizenship. To prove loyalty to his new country, the eldest son William, a farmer and weaver by trade, enlisted in Captain James Vaughn's company of infantry during the War of 1812.

Nathan Jr., who was W. A.'s father, bought a modest farm. He married the former Susannah Heath Cureton, and they became the parents of seven children. Eliza was born in 1814, John Cureton in 1815, James Young in 1817, Mary Young in 1819. William Addison (W.A.), the Civil War soldier, was born Sunday, April 28, 1822; Susannah Cureton in 1827, and Thomas Taylor Cureton in 1831.

During the Second Seminole War of the late 1830s, James enlisted in an infantry unit and was immediately ordered to Florida to help quell the Indian uprising. When he returned to South Carolina, his stories of a wild new frontier with its bounty of available, virgin land, remained with W. A. and his oldest brother John C. They both realized good farmland was hard to come by in South Carolina, where years of steady cotton production had nearly exhausted the red soil.

The two brothers married sisters. John C. wed Rosannah Young and W. A. married her younger sister, Rebecca Caroline Young, daughters of Thompson Young and the granddaughters of James Abraham Young, an Irish immigrant from County Down, Ireland. By 1850 Rebecca had already given birth to four children on the small farm where they lived. They were Melissa born in 1844, William Young in 1845, Susannah Heath in 1848, and Thompson Calhoun in the early months of 1850. John Quitman in 1852, and Thompson Hayne Pearce born in 1855, added to the family. The 1850 Slave Census shows that W. A. owned two young slaves, one, a mulatto male, age nineteen, and the second a black female, age eighteen.

W. A.'s brother John C. moved to Florida in 1855, settling at Alligator (the present Lake City). Restless and discontented with life back in Newberry County, W. A. followed. His family arrived in Columbia County near his brother in December 1856, after a long and arduous journey over rugged roads and hazardous trails. Newnansville, the nearest settlement, located in nearby northern Alachua County, was the center of cotton and vegetable-growing country. Once settled on his eight hundred acres, W. A. and his twelve-year-old son, Young, and the increasing slave force they had acquired, began clearing pine barrens for planting.

The family was completed with the births of Martha Arabella, nicknamed Belle, Barnwell Rhett, Estelle, and Willie Annie, who was born in August of 1864 while her father was fighting for the Confederacy south of Petersburg, Virginia.

W. A. was an ardent supporter of the Confederacy when the war started in the spring of 1861. In fact, for many years preceding the war, he had been a firm proponent of state rights who gave his children names like Calhoun, John Quitman, Hayne Pearce, and Barnwell Rhett, all Southern fire-eaters. Although a loyal advocate of Southern independence, W. A. refrained from joining the war until Confederate conscription laws forced him to enlist in 1863. He was forty-one years old. Young, W. A.'s oldest son, was sixteen when the first shot sounded, but in December 1863 he turned eighteen, and by law he had to be mustered into Confederate ranks.

John C. never joined the army—he was past the legal conscript age of forty-five. His sons Thompson, Nathan and William Marcus all served gallantly in various Florida infantry and militia units. Rebecca and Rosannah also had two brothers living in Lake City, James E. Young and Joseph Young, and both men donned Confederate uniforms to fight for the Southern cause. Joseph Young, a prodigious letter writer, belonged to the same battalion as W. A. and Young.

W. A., a self-educated man, was also a consummate letter writer, often writing two expansive letters a day from the trenches of Petersburg. These letters form a strong backbone of the story of the Florida regiment whose career is followed in the book.

ANTEBELLUM FLORIDA TO SECESSION

At the time of the Civil War, Florida, which had entered the Union in 1845, was split into three geographic sections. West Florida extended from the Apalachicola River to the western part of what is called the "panhandle" of Florida; Middle Florida included the rich farmlands between the Apalachicola to the Suwannee Rivers; and East Florida embodied all land east of the Suwannee to the Atlantic Ocean. By 1855, just ten years after her entry into the Union, Florida had seen staggering growth rates more than doubling the state's population. South Florida, a land of odd mangrove swamps and mosquitoes, opened up slowly and drew some pioneering settlers too.

There were, of course, disadvantages to this land of eternal sunshine. Planters and yeoman farmers were always at the mercy of huge storms. In 1858 a hurricane roared through North Florida dousing the fields with torrential rains, soaking and ruining cotton and industrial machinery and farm implements. Still, settlers flocked to Florida with its promised wealth and independent spirit.

Florida's economy prior to the war depended primarily upon agriculture. The state boasted a variety of crops of which cotton was king. Corn and cereal grains such as wheat, oats, rye, and barley were grown throughout northern Florida. On a smaller scale, sweet potatoes, arrowroot, indigo, cochineal, silk, and olives were also cultivated. Tobacco emerged as a widespread cash crop, and along the coastal hamlets rice provided staple food for families and slaves as well as becoming an export crop. Grapes and exotic citrus fruits like oranges, lemons, and pomegranates provided interesting variety, along with sugar cane. Every farmer also owned cattle, hogs, and sheep.

While most settlers were small farmers, Florida boasted a planting class also, especially in the cotton-rich belt of Middle and Eastern Florida, where frontier slaves were used to clear the land for the cultivation of cotton.

From the outset, Florida was destined to be a slave state. Her sentiments concerning property (defined as slavery) wholly and emphatically aligned with the philosophy of the South. By 1860 there were

5,152 slaveholders in Florida, of whom only 808 owned twenty or more slaves. Most of the small farmers whose lands adjoined the slave plantation aspired to owning slaves, if they had not yet acquired one or two.

Out of necessity, the plantation owners taught their slaves a trade. Slaves became carpenters, blacksmiths, wheelwrights, and masons whom their masters often hired out to others. On large plantations slaves were kept in separate quarters. The small farmers, on the other hand, worked alongside their slaves in the fields. Often slaves ate meals with their masters and were considered part of the family. Many farmers, such as W. A. Hunter, cared for and were fond of their slaves.

The coastal waters teemed with fish to be caught by the local fishermen. The popular eating fish were sheephead, grouper, and the ubiquitous mullet. These fish were either sold fresh in local markets or salted and pickled in casks, then shipped inland where they became the mainstay of many slaves' diet.

Although salted pork was the foundation of the Floridian's diet, beef from cattle was growing in popularity. During the 1850s the cattle industry in Florida emerged, and Florida rivaled Texas in beef production. Cattle were driven for miles across the prairies of southwestern Florida to ports for shipping to northern markets. The river valleys of the Myakka, Caloosahatchee, Peace, and Kissimmee Rivers were the primary ranging areas. By late 1863, Florida's cattle industry proved to be a major supplier of beef for the Confederate army in Tennessee.

The vast pine forests of the panhandle provided a lucrative lumber industry. Pine trees were felled and the wood was used to satisfy the growing demand for building supplies. Turpentine was also manufactured from the lumber and sold throughout the south.

Other industries began to flourish in pre-war Florida. Salt was extracted from evaporated seawater along the Gulf coast near Cedar Key. Cotton mills and sawmills were established in northern Florida, and banking emerged successfully following the financially insecure banking era of the Territorial period. Finally, during the 1850s, as railroads reached Florida, the metropolitan areas of St. Augustine and Jacksonville began to see visitors during winter months. These early tourists were both Northerners and Southerners seeking the balmy breezes of the coastal cities.

Politically Florida was thoroughly Southern from the inception of statehood. On April 9, 1860, the Democratic Party of Florida held its annual convention and overwhelmingly approved the institution of Negro slavery as a necessity, declaring Congress "must protect it in the territories." Democrats favoring secession controlled the political machine within the state. Sixteen of the largest newspapers heralded these radical politicians. Those men opposing secession, such as former territorial governor Richard Keith Call, were labeled submissionists and "Union Shriekers." Some were beaten and shamefully driven from the state.

On June 4, 1860, a second Democratic convention was held and John Milton was nominated as candidate for governor. He was an extremist and a fire-eater, a true advocate of John C. Calhoun's doctrine of nullification. He held the fervent belief that an individual state maintained a special right to withdraw its allegiance to the Union if that state felt its personal interests were seriously infringed upon. John Milton defeated Edward Hopkins of the Constitutional Union Party, becoming Florida's controversial wartime governor.

Public sentiment heavily favored secession during the month prior to the pivotal presidential election of 1860. Senator David Yulee declared, "if the modern Republicans succeed in acquiring possession of the Federal Government, it will be the duty of the Southern State to secede." At the Democratic Party meeting in Gainesville, the conservatives boldly warned, "if in consequence of northern fanaticism the irrepressible conflict must come we are prepared to meet it."

Anxieties ran high as the November election of 1860 neared. On October 5 lame-duck Governor Madison Starke Perry admitted that Florida would not take the lead in seceding from the Union, but would be eager to follow the lead of another. On election day presidential candidate John C. Breckenridge swept the majority of Florida's vote. As the parties printed separate ballots, there was no Republican Party in Florida and Abraham Lincoln did not receive a single vote. Lincoln carried the Northern States and won the bid for Presidency, ominously foreshadowing the conflict to come.

With their future threatened, Floridians spoke out with decisive passion. In Waldo a town meeting was called for November 8, and the citizens pledged to "march to the assistance of the first state that may secede." They further proclaimed their intentions by burning Abe

Lincoln in effigy the following day. The headline of the Fernandina *East Floridian* on November 14, 1860, summed up popular sentiment with the masthead—"The Secession of the State of Florida, The Dissolution of the Union, The Formation of a Southern Confederacy." In Ocala a new flag was unfurled with a single blue star and "Let Us Alone" inscribed across the face. In Quincy a banner was raised with the inscription "Secession, Florida, Sovereignty, Independence." Inflamed over the election, Governor Perry stated from Tallahassee, "The crisis expected by men of observation and reflection has at last come. The only hope that the Southern states have for domestic peace or for future respect of property is dependent on secession from faithless, perjured confederates."

The Secessionists gained further credibility in mid-December when the Florida Baptists met at their state convention in Monticello and voted to back secession. The body resolved, "cordial sympathy with, and hearty approbation of those who are determined to maintain the integrity of the Southern States, even by a disruption of all existing political ties." Even the church supported secession now. All Florida had to do was wait for the first bold state to secede, then firmly follow.

South Carolina took that step on December 20, 1860. On January 10, 1861, after deliberating for one week, Florida voted, sixty-two to seven, in favor of secession. By this time Mississippi had already joined South Carolina in breaking ties with the Union. The news of dissolution caused a wave of excitement to surge through Tallahassee. Enthusiastic crowds mobbed the streets, dancing and celebrating the great victory. After sundown, torch-lit parades streamed through the city proclaiming with shouts and the clanging of bells that Florida was freed from Yankee aggression. Church bells rang in St. Augustine where a new flag, displaying a palmetto palm and an eagle resting on a globe with the state's motto "Let Us Alone" clenched in its mouth, was hoisted up the flagpole in the plaza, near the public market. Large bonfires were lit in Madison, where bells were rung and cannon were fired. Proud men predicted an end of hostilities within two months and the haughty dared to "drink all the blood that will be spilt." The next day Governor-elect John Milton unfurled Florida's official flag, a white banner containing three stars for the first three states to secede.

Florida plantation owners and the more numerous small, independence-minded farmers flocked to buy the banners. Joining these first eager (and unknowing) Rebel Floridians were W. A. and Young Hunter—the conscriptees. Their personal story told here will stand for the story of all the rest of the frontier Floridians who added their strength to the Southern cause.

2.

FLORIDA AND THE BEGINNING OF THE WAR

At the time Florida seceded from the Union, she was a growing frontier state barely sixteen years old, with a population of 140,000, of whom nearly half were black slaves. Of the remaining 70,000 only a fraction were adult, white male citizens eligible to vote. Prior to secession, 12,800 men were legal voters in Florida, amounting to less than ten percent of the total population.[1]

Florida was in a precarious position from the start. Its coastline stretched 1,150 miles and demanded large military forces to repel threats of Union raiding parties. On January 10, 1861, the day after Mississippi seceded and the day before Alabama's secession, Florida parted peacefully from the Union. Lame-duck Governor Madison Starke Perry was then faced with the problem of forcing the existing Federal troops out of arsenals and forts within the state's boundaries.

In January 1861 Federals were occupying Forts Barrancas, McRae, and Pickens in Pensacola Bay, Fort Clinch in Fernandina on Amelia Island, Fort Marion in St. Augustine, Fort Taylor and the Barracks in Key West, lesser forts in Garden Key in the Dry Tortugas, and a small arsenal of arms and munitions strategically located at Chattahoochee on the Apalachicola River. Five days prior to secession, Florida Senator David Yulee urged his friend Joseph Finegan to occupy all Federal arsenals and forts located within the state. Yulee maintained that these forts were built to protect Florida and were the property of the state. The state acted promptly. By January 7 Forts Clinch and Marion were in Florida's hands.[2]

The following day, Lieutenant Adam J. Slemmer, commanding the Federal contingent in Pensacola Bay, realized it was tactically impossible to defend Forts Barrancas and McRae due to their vulnerability to overland assaults. During the dark, quiet morning hours of January 8, Lieutenant Slemmer abandoned the two strategically inferior forts, destroying 20,000 pounds of powder in the process. He hastily retired his command to the more formidable Fort Pickens on the western tip of Santa Rosa Island. Elsewhere, arsenals and forts were handed over to state officials peaceably. Only Fort Pickens and Key West remained in Federal hands throughout the war.[3]

Although Fort Pickens remained a Union stronghold, it did not go unchallenged. Both state and Confederate governments repeatedly demanded Federal abandonment. On October 8, 1861, the Confederates formulated a plan to invade Santa Rosa Island to dislodge Federal troops stationed in the garrison. A Southern force of 1,000 men commanded by Richard Henry Anderson of South Carolina converged on Pensacola. The force consisted of troops from Georgia, Alabama, and the First Florida Infantry, commanded by Colonel James Patton Anderson. Also included were independent companies from Georgia and one artillery company.[4]

At two o'clock the following morning, the Confederate force invaded Santa Rosa Island. Immediately, they overran a camp of New York Zouaves, driving them away at bayonet point and setting the camp ablaze. The advancement was eventually checked, and the Rebels were forced to retreat from the island. Casualties were extremely high on both sides, but clearly the Southern force suffered the greatest loss. Federal losses were fourteen dead, thirty-six wounded, and twenty captured, while the Confederates lost twenty-eight men dead, thirty-nine wounded, and thirty captured. Florida suffered a sizable share of these casualties. The First Florida Regiment absorbed six killed, eight wounded, and twelve captured.[5]

With the advent of the Civil War, the demand for beef to feed parts of the Confederate army magnified. Texas cattle were the "beeves" of choice. However, with the fall of Vicksburg in July 1863, the channels to Texas beef were abruptly closed. The Union owned the Mississippi River; thus, the Confederate Commissary needed to look elsewhere to supply her hungry army. General Braxton Bragg's army required an average of 400,000 meat rations per month. The logical source was Florida, as her supply of the mangy "scrub" cattle seemed inexhaustible. General Bragg grew dependent on Florida cattle, forcing the state to become the Confederacy's principal source of meat supply.[6]

The large herds of northern Florida were secured initially. But as the need for more heads grew, the cattle drives started further south along the peninsula until they reached Southwest Florida. It was imperative to keep the channels of beef open to the Confederacy. Numerous independent militia companies were formed. Their objective was not only to protect the state from enemy intrusion, but also to protect Florida's cattle interests.

But the main goal of the Confederacy in Florida, of course, was enlisting men to fight its war for independence. Governor Perry appointed Joseph Finegan of Fernandina to be director of state military affairs with the sole responsibility of organizing independent militia units. "Old Barney," as he was called, was born on November 17, 1814, at Clones in County Monaghan, Ireland. At age twenty he immigrated to Florida. In 1837 he married the widow Rebecca Travers, who had three daughters from her previous marriage. Joseph and Rebecca became the parents of three additional children, two sons and one daughter. Finegan and his family lived in St. Augustine until 1851 when they moved up the coast to Jacksonville, where Finegan opened a lumber mill and ran a mercantile business. Both endeavors prospered and by 1855 he had moved his family to the Fernandina area and built a plantation on Amelia Island.[7]

During these years he befriended David L. Yulee, the future U. S. Senator, and together they founded the Florida Railroad Company, linking the Atlantic and Gulf coasts of Florida. Their company made small fortunes for them.[8]

Finegan, an Irish Anglican devoted to his faith, made sure each of his children received an excellent education. At age forty-five in 1860, Finegan was described as "jovial and hearty." He was a wealthy and influential man strongly entrenched in the Southern philosophy of life when he represented Nassau County at the State Democratic Convention in 1860.[9]

Generals Robert E. Lee and P.G.T. Beauregard duly praised Finegan for his organizational skills as director of state military affairs. In 1862 Confederate Senator David Yulee requested a command for his friend. Governor Milton objected on the grounds that Finegan was unqualified for military command. Jefferson Davis overruled Milton's objectives and appointed Finegan as brigadier general in command of the district of Middle and East Florida. While Finegan was in command, Union troops occupied Jacksonville three separate times. On two occasions his plantation on Amelia Island was sacked and his slaves ran free. The behavior of his slaves forever embittered General Finegan and proved to be a determining factor in the way he treated Black Union soldiers.[10]

Following the appointment of Joseph Finegan as director of state military affairs, the call went out for the formation of militia units to protect Florida. Many of the existing independent militias consolidated, forming state infantry regiments to serve in the Confederate army. The First Regiment was mustered in early summer of 1861 and earned praise for its effort in the futile attempt to take Santa Rosa Island. In March 1862, the First Regiment was ordered to Corinth, Mississippi, where it served the duration of the conflict in the western theater. The Second Florida Regiment consisted of independent companies from all over the state. The Second mustered into Confederate service July 13, 1861, at Lavilla, near Jacksonville, and two days later was sent north to Virginia. The Third Regiment mustered on August 10, 1861, at Amelia Island and served in Florida until ordered to Chattanooga in August 1862. The Fourth Regiment was organized from ten independent companies in May 1862, and quickly moved up to General Braxton Bragg's Army in Tennessee.[11]

The Fifth Regiment mustered into Confederate service in 1862 and was immediately sent to Virginia, just in time to defend against Union General McClellan's Peninsular Campaign. The Sixth Florida Regiment organized in the early spring 1862 was also sent to Bragg's Army. The Seventh Regiment was organized in April 1862 at Gainesville and was commanded by former Governor Perry. The Seventh was also sent to Bragg's Army. Finally the Eighth Florida Regiment mustered in May 1862 and was hastily shipped north to Richmond.[12]

The Ninth Florida would be a conglomerate. An important unit of what would become the Ninth Florida, and the focal point of our study, was Stewart's company. In December 1862 Asa A. Stewart received permission from the Secretary of War, Jonathan Withers, to raise a company of men "over the conscript age forty-five years for service in the State of Florida, and not to be attached to any regiment or battalion." The purpose of this company of militia volunteers was specifically to provide local defense and assistance. Before his commission Stewart had been a farmer in Welborn in Columbia County.[13]

He owned one hundred thirty-five acres, but only thirty-five acres had been cleared for cultivation. In 1860 his farm had been valued at

$800. Stewart was not a large slaveholder either, owning only six slaves. Stewart had a large family and an illiterate wife named Nancy.[14]

On February 11, 1863, fifty-year-old Stewart was elected captain of his fledgling independent company. Following his election to captain, he enrolled thirty-eight new conscripts. By the end of February Stewart's company had grown to include sixty-six men. Enrollment dropped dramatically through the winter and spring, but picked up again in August when thirty-two inductees were enrolled. Twenty-five more enrolled in September. By October 1, 1863, Stewart's company numbered one hundred sixty-six men.[15]

In addition to Stewart, two other men were over forty-five years old. They were Brevet Lieutenant Isaac Wiley and Private John Rowan. Five boys under age eighteen years were also mustered into the company: Jasper Curl, John Green, William McAllen and Miles Yeomans were seventeen years old, while John Prevatt, whose father and three older brothers were also enrolled in Stewart's company, was the youngest boy in the ranks at sixteen years of age.[16]

W. A. Hunter, whose letters tell the story of Stewart's independent militia as well as the (consolidated) Ninth Florida Regiment, joined Stewart's company in 1863. Hunter was enrolled in Lake City by Major R. B. Thomas on Friday, August 7. Fortunately for W. A., Stewart's company was based in Lake City about thirteen miles north of his farm, which enabled him to make quick trips home when leave could be obtained.[17]

When W. A. enlisted in Stewart's independent company, he was forty-one years old. As a private he drew a salary of $11.00 per month. Throughout the war W. A. never seemed to suffer a lack of money because Rebecca was able to send it upon his request. Stewart's militia company remained headquartered in Lake City, serving under Brigadier General Joseph Finegan, who commanded the District of East Florida.[18]

During February, Stewart's company patrolled the area around Lake City, and in early March, the company experienced its first taste of action. Along with additional independent companies from Northern Florida, Stewart's company was ordered to Camp Finegan, eight miles west of Jacksonville. Federal gunboats were patrolling the St. Johns River, and Confederate scouts reported that five enemy transports loaded with Negro soldiers had landed and occupied the city.

It was the Confederates' mission to confront the enemy and "cut off, capture, or kill their pickets." Twice the small Florida force assaulted Union lines with steadfast bravery driving them back under fire. The enemy abandoned its position but set Jacksonville ablaze before evacuating it. The groups of independent companies comprising the Confederate force fought the fire and were successful in preserving a few important buildings. The bravery of the new companies did not go unheralded—they received commendations for high conduct during "severe, constant and dangerous action."[19]

Stewart's company remained at Camp Finegan through March and while there mustered five men into the outfit. After leaving Camp Finegan, they returned to Lake City, the headquarters for the military district of East Florida. There, the company was charged with such duties as enrolling conscripts, interning or guarding captured Union soldiers, and scouting the countryside to gather up Confederate Army stragglers and renegade bands of Rebel deserters who were filtering into the less populated counties from the northern battlefields.[20]

In July Captain Stewart split his company into four detachments. The first and largest contingent was detailed to guard the strategic Columbus Railroad Bridge spanning the Suwannee River thirty miles west of Lake City. The second group was detached to the Sanderson supply center where all army provisions were stored. These troops served as guards to the commissary and also acted as teamsters, hauling goods by wagon train. The third group served as provost marshals guarding the arsenal and powder magazine in Lake City. The fourth detachment's duty was split between guarding prisoners in Lake City and scouting the countryside.[21]

The exact number of soldiers posted at each detachment is unknown because muster rolls fail to disclose all the soldiers' whereabouts. However, it is known that some of these soldiers served in multiple areas over the course of many months. The rolls show thirty-eight men were stationed at Columbus Bridge, twenty-one men served in the commissary at Sanderson and twenty-three were provost marshals in Lake City. Not a single muster record documents the existence of the contingency serving as prisoner guards. Although the individual records fail to record the existence of this detachment, its existence is known through the writing of W. A. Hunter. W. A. recorded in a letter written February 19, 1864, "We started at six o'clock with our prisoners. We were taken them to jail."[22]

To raise an efficient fighting force in the district of East Florida, Brigadier General Joseph Finegan was ordered to organize a battalion of independent companies.[23]

The companies comprising what was to be the Sixth Florida Battalion were to remain separate bodies, each guarding its own appointed section of northern Florida stretching from Columbus to Jacksonville to Tampa. Captain Stewart's company, officially called Company E, remained in the four units which had been organized earlier. However, because of the growing size of the company, on October 1, 1863, seventy-seven men were separated from Stewart's company to join Captain Benjamin L. Reynolds' Company H. Reynolds previously had served as a sergeant in Stewart's company. The majority of the men who joined Company H were from neighboring Baker County; those remaining with Stewart were, of course, from Columbia County.[24]

On December 29, 1863, Young Hunter turned eighteen. Even though he was needed to run the farm, by Confederate conscription laws he was forced to join the army. On the first day of the New Year, Young journeyed into Lake City, just as his father had done five months before, and was sworn into the same company as his father by Captain Stewart himself. Youthful, green, and impetuous, Young was eager for military service. Fortunately for W. A., Young was in his outfit and the father was able to keep a protective eye on his son.[25]

3.

THE ROOTS OF THE NINTH FLORIDA

In the continued effort to raise an efficient fighting force in the district of East Florida, the Confederate command directed General Joseph Finegan to organize a battalion drawn from local independent companies including Captain Stewart's. Coastal areas such as St. Augustine were lost to Union possession early in the war and many Floridians feared that a Federal attempt to drive inland and capture the state capital at Tallahassee was inevitable. Therefore, formation of a powerful aggregate battalion was thought necessary to provide adequate security within the state. On September 11, 1863, the Sixth Florida Battalion, consisting of seven companies and three independent militia-type companies, was formed. President Davis appointed John M. Martin commander the same day the Sixth Battalion was organized.[1]

John Martin was born in South Carolina in 1832. He received two years of military training at the Citadel in Charleston, leaving before completing his courses. In 1856 he removed to Ocala located in Marion County, Florida, where he established himself as a planter. When the call to arms echoed throughout the South, Martin responded by raising the Marion Light Artillery Company, and he was elected captain. During the summer of 1862 his company joined General Edward Kirby Smith's army in Tennessee and participated in the Battle of Richmond, Kentucky, on August 30. His company fought bravely, but Martin was seriously wounded in the battle and was forced to retire for medical aid. When he was physically able to travel, Martin returned home to recuperate from his wounds. While in Florida he was elected as a state representative to the Confederate Congress, where he served until the following year.[2]

Desiring to return to the field of action, Martin declined a bid for re-election in 1863. The President commissioned him lieutenant colonel and gave him command of the newly formed Sixth Florida Battalion. He was unable to assume command until his term in Congress expired; consequently, Major Pickens Bird commanded the Sixth Battalion from September 11, until Martin arrived on November 1, 1863.

The Sixth Florida Battalion was comprised of ten companies. Asa A. Stewart's independent company, with the Hunters, became Company E. Other units were Company A, the "Gulf Coast Rangers" commanded by Captain John C. Chambers; Company B, the "Oklawaha Rangers" led by the colorful Captain John W. Pearson; Company C, the "Brooksville Guards" under Samuel E. Hope; Company D, the "B. F. Guards" with John Bryan; Company F, Alfred F. D. P. Mooty leader; Company G, Captain Summerfield M. G. Gary; Company H, led by Benjamin L. Reynolds; Company I, James McNeil commander; and Company K commanded by Jacob C. Eichelberger. These companies patrolled a triangular area of northern Florida stretching from Columbus to Jacksonville to Tampa.

Florida boasted colorful personalities during the war just as other Southern states did and the Ninth even more so. Captain John W. Pearson of Company B, the "Oklawaha Rangers," was an interesting example. "The Oklawaha Rangers" were mustered into service at Camp McCarthy on the banks of the Oklawaha River in Putnam County May 14, 1862. On this date seventy-one men were enrolled and fifty-two-year-old John W. Pearson was elected captain. The men's ages varied from six privates who were seventeen years of age to Private Andrew Wells and Captain Pearson both age fifty-two, but the average age was twenty-six. By the end of the war the Oklawaha Rangers had enrolled a total of one hundred fifty-six men.[3]

Although Pearson's company officially organized in May, it had existed previously as a local militia unit protecting the town of Palatka on the St. Johns River. Following the sinking of the sailing yacht "America" in Dunn's Lake, southeast of Palatka, Union forces tried to raise the ship. The Oklawaha Rangers were sent to Dunn's Creek, which feeds the lake, on March 28, 1862, with orders to fill the creek with trees in an effort to block the only exit to the St. Johns. After scouting the eastern shore of the St. Johns, Captain Pearson decided to make the sixteen-mile crossing in two separate detachments during the middle of the night. When morning came, he found the enemy had vanished, so Pearson and his men then proceeded to the nearby plantation of Dr. May.

The captain planned to engage the enemy force of two hundred men there, but the Federal troops refused to fight. Pearson sent a small band of his men to coax the "Yankees out of the thick woods" and into a fight. After failing to interest the enemy in battle, Captain Pearson took out his anger and frustration by arresting several whites and Blacks and charging them with being Union sympathizers. He even hung one of Dr. May's Negroes. After returning to Camp McCarthy, Pearson complained to his superiors that a small Confederate force was not safe on the eastern shore of the St. Johns, claiming there was a constant "risk of betrayal." According to Pearson, all problems could be solved if only martial law was proclaimed and "many suspects hung."[4]

Captain Pearson, a wizened old man, called himself a "guerrilla in every sense of the word." He was a firm disciplinarian, assembling his men by trumpeting a cow's horn. He never backed away from a fight, nor was he afraid to battle when the odds heavily favored the enemy. As an example, shortly after muster, the company was sent to Fort Brooke near Tampa with an order to hold his position. Pearson suffered from a scarcity of guns and requisitioned additional guns and cannon. Due to the paucity of artillery guns in East Florida, the requisition was not honored. Nevertheless, the guerrilla Pearson held the fort through guile and efficient leadership.[5]

In late June 1862, a Federal gunboat anchored broadside of Fort Brooke and opened her cannon ports. The ship lowered a launch and twenty men, including a lieutenant bearing a flag of truce, rowed toward shore. Pearson boarded a boat with eighteen men and met his foe upon the waters of Tampa Bay, determined not to let the Federals ashore. The Union officer demanded Pearson unconditionally surrender the fort. The captain defiantly declared, "There is no such letter in our book, we don't surrender." The lieutenant answered with a threat to commence firing on the fort at six o'clock the same evening. Pearson remarked, "pitch in." Three rousing Rebel yells were voiced by the captain's men. Each boat returned to its respective placement. Pearson began evacuating the women and children; then he moved what cannon he had one mile to the rear, aiming them at the ship in the harbor.

The Union cannonading started promptly at six o'clock. The gunboat fired twenty salvos, one of which landed in the fort commons, but failed to explode, and Pearson answered with twenty-two shots. Residents of Tampa reported that Pearson's guns had struck the Federal ship. The following morning firing commenced at ten o'clock and lasted till noon. Captain Pearson kept his ground and proved he meant to stay by hoisting the Confederate flag. The Captain boasted of the flag, "It seemed to float so proudly and beautifully." This act infuriated the frustrated Federals. They fired two successive salvos then weighed anchor and left Pearson "in peaceful possession of the town that they that evening before demanded unconditional surrender in such furioso-gusto manner."[6]

On two separate occasions in late October 1862, Federal gunboats fired upon the civilians of Tampa and the Oklawaha Rangers. Although there were narrow escapes, no one was hurt, but these actions disgusted Pearson. On Saturday, December 13, two Federal gunboats slipped into Tampa Bay and rammed a large blockade-runner within sight of the garrison. The following day the ships left, but on March 27, 1863, a Federal gunboat reappeared before the fort. Pearson avenged the abused civilians of Tampa with a plan that was to be the highlight of his Confederate military career.[7]

Pearson ordered a detachment of his men to paint themselves black, pose as Negro slaves, and paddle out in a small boat keeping a safe distance from the enemy ship. The men concealed their weapons in the boat, began paddling, and when they were within earshot of the ship, they called for help. The ship's captain, thinking they were a band of fugitive slaves seeking sanctuary, sent out a party of twenty-six men in a yawl to rescue the Negroes. The ruse was successful. When the two skiffs met, Pearson's men brandished their weapons and slaughtered all but two men who managed to escape. Indeed Captain Pearson proved to be a guerrilla fighter of the most creative type. Such was the experience of the highly individualistic B Company of the Sixth Florida.[8]

Columbus, a small Florida town, was situated on the eastern bank of the Suwannee River approximately thirty miles west of Lake City. It was a strategic point, since Columbus was a terminus on the Florida Atlantic & Gulf Railroad, and it had the only railroad bridge leading to Tallahassee. It was here that a detachment of Captain Asa A. Stewart's company was posted to protect East Florida from enemy infiltration and to insure that a supply and communication line with the capitol remained open. It was also at Columbus that a separate group of local men organized into an independent company, calling themselves the "B. F. Guards," also eventually to be part of the Sixth Florida.

Company D, the B. F. Guards, mustered into Confederate service October 6, 1862. On the same day fifty-two-year-old John Bryan was elected captain of the company and his younger brother, forty-six-year-old Joseph D. Bryan was appointed second lieutenant. Bryan was elected captain because of his ability to drill and discipline a green military unit. On the day of organization sixty-nine men enrolled in the B. F. Guards. By the war's end twice as many men had mustered into the company. Although the numbers totaled 138 men, the average daily aggregate was considerably less. The median age stood higher than that of the previous independent companies, fixed at thirty-two years. Ages ranged from Musician J. B. Crews and Private Francis Roberts, who were only fourteen, to elderly men such as Private Alex Crews, sixty-three, C. F. McCall, sixty-four, and seventy-two-year-old Private Silas Hunter, no relation to W. A.[9]

Captain Bryan kept his men posted at Columbus Bridge the first few months following organization, and on January 21, 1863, his company was so inadequately supplied that Bryan was compelled to remark, "My company, having yet received no accoutrement is destitute." On March 1, 1863, the B. F. Guards received orders to proceed to Camp Finegan. In July while still posted at Camp Finegan, forty-nine-year-old First Lieutenant James T. Padgett fell ill and was placed on sick furlough June 30. Finally, by July 16, realizing his health was unstable, he resigned his commission.[10]

In September the B. F. Guards, Company D of the Sixth Florida, relocated to Green Cove Springs, south of Jacksonville on the St. Johns River, where they remained until the end of December. During this time both Captain Bryan and his brother Joseph resigned because of ill health complicated by advanced age. James F. Tucker, a short, prematurely gray-haired, twenty-two-year-old man, who once had attended the Marietta Military Academy, replaced Bryan as captain. He had been given the task of drilling and disciplining the company the previous month. Because of his training Tucker was promoted from second lieutenant directly to captain and led his company to Virginia. In November the company returned to Camp Finegan and stayed posted there until they were forced to retreat on February 8, 1864.[11]

W. A.'s brother-in-law, Joseph A. Young, was a sergeant in Company D. Joseph's service in the Confederacy originated with his July 13, 1861, enrollment into Company L, "The Madison Rangers," of the Second Florida Regiment. He enlisted as a private and soon was promoted to first sergeant. He followed his regiment north to Virginia and fought valiantly in the Peninsular campaign during the spring of 1862. Union forces captured him. As a prisoner of war, Joseph was exchanged for one Levi Lee on March 1, 1863, and returned to Florida. On June 3, 1863, he transferred to Captain Bryan's company holding his previous rank of first sergeant;[12] thus, he too would be part of the new Sixth Florida.

Following the formation of the Sixth Florida Battalion, most of the companies involved were concentrated west of Jacksonville. Other companies and detachments were posted at strategic locations along vital railroad lines and bridges or critical waterways protecting the military headquarters at Lake City, as well as the fertile interior farm land from possible enemy landings and assaults. On occasion situations arose that required the consolidation of a some of these companies into one viable fighting force. One such incident happened on October 12, 1863, when General Finegan was granted permission to gather "all the force" available to enter Taylor County and "capture, slay, or destroy" the rising number of deserters and Yankees hiding there.[13]

Yankee sympathizers were always a problem. In Jacksonville, Pensacola, Tampa, and even St. Augustine, the oldest city in the United States, and in coastal towns and settlements, the sympathies tended to favor the Union. Captain John W. Pearson of the Oklawaha Rangers had complained that a small Confederate force was not safe on the eastern shore of the St. Johns River, claiming there is a constant "risk of betrayal." According to Captain Pearson, all problems could be solved if only martial law was proclaimed and "many suspects hung."[14]

Union sympathies in the coastal hamlets remained a nuisance for the Confederacy throughout the war. The greatest interior threat to Florida, however, proved to be Confederate deserters. At the beginning of hostilities in April 1861, the fledgling Confederate government found it easy to fill the ranks of her emerging armies as volunteers were eager to sign up. Promotion of the "Southern cause," frenzy, and boastful talk of a quick end to the war proved to be the South's best recruiting tools. Early in the war, the situation appeared rosy for the Confederacy. However, by 1862, the Southern army, having been depleted by casualties and disease, found it imperative to induct those who had not yet volunteered.

Acting expediently to fill her shrinking ranks, the Confederate Congress passed the Conscription Act of 1862. Although this act served its purpose by increasing the size of the military, it drove those who vowed never to enter the service into the inland swamps and forests where they waited out the war.

These holdouts, often Northern sympathizers themselves, were determined not to serve and banded together in the wilderness sections of Lafayette, Walton, Taylor, Levy and Washington counties in West Florida. Governor John Milton described the situation in West Florida as, "in bad condition for our cause. The disloyal are in touch with the enemy." Disloyalty ran so rampant that Governor Milton stated, "The sheriff of Washington County and others are now in the service of the enemy." Additionally, there was a concentration of deserters interspersed in the southwest part of Florida stretching from Tampa Bay to Fort Myers. Surprisingly large numbers of Confederate deserters from the armies in Tennessee and Virginia sought refuge and were openly accepted by the holdouts. Runaway slaves were also welcomed into these folds.[15]

The majority of the holdouts, deserters, and Negroes were poor and illiterate. A young lad from Madison County wrote his mother illustrating the sentiment exhibited by his class of citizens.

Seat my Self this Morning to inform you that I am Well and we have got orders to leave here But I do not Know where we are going to but out west I will wright to you as soon as I git to my Journey end...Wright to me [if] Brother Ben is gone back to Virginia and Tell Him if He Haint Gone Not Go Take the Woods First.[16]

By 1863, droves of deserters numbering in the thousands hid themselves in the dense Florida swamps. Raging discontent in Southern ranks prompted mass desertions. Many reasons drove these men to desperation: lack of food, fatigue, filth and disease, irregular pay, and other hardships played heavily into decision-making. Often the Union blockaders aided the refugee bands and encouraged them to raid local farmers and to steal their bounty. The refugee bands grew powerful. In late 1863, one such band located in Taylor County organized itself into a company called the "Independent Union Rangers." The group even drafted a constitution signed by all thirty-five of its original members. The constitution's provisions included true allegiance to the United States of America, absolute obedience to their officers, execution of proven spies, just division of the spoils, complete secrecy concerning the Rangers, and the death penalty for any member who deserted the band.[17]

Early on they contented themselves with petty raiding for sustenance, but as the war progressed, these refugee bands grew more aggressive. By 1864 these bands aided the Union by ambushing Confederate military patrols, raiding plantations and cattle ranches, stealing and slaughtering cattle, stealing Negroes, and upsetting general law and order in Southern-sympathizing territory. Often their pillaging forays ended near coastal areas where Confederate reconnaissance intelligence was passed on to the waiting Union blockade commanders.

In addition to terrorizing the citizenry, the stealing of slaves from the prominent cotton planters was proving to be more than a mere nuisance. In 1864 planters moved their slaves inland to prevent the possible loss of valuable property. On June 18, the *Gainesville Cotton States* warned, "The deserters are now carrying on an organized attempt to steal every negro they can in an effort to ruin the county." The editor feared that all would be lost east of the Suwannee River if the Confederacy did not organize and fight back. "East Florida must make up its mind whether to fight or submit to the deserters."[18]

Florida and the Confederacy needed to fight to retain law and order and to maintain stable peace and confidence among the citizenry. More importantly, these deserters hiding in the dark swamps needed to be apprehended and returned to the Southern ranks where manpower was desperately lacking.

In September 1863, Brigadier General Joseph Finegan, commanding Middle and East Florida, sent Confederate States Marshal E. E. Blackburn into the swamps in Taylor County. Finegan charged Blackburn with full authority to grant amnesty to all deserters, with the intent that "they be allowed to join organizations in Florida not exceeding 4 in any one company." Marshal Blackburn was unsuccessful in his efforts to obtain an interview. On October 5, Judge John C. McGehee of Madison, aghast at the brazen attitude of the deserters, wrote to General Finegan, requesting that the general send a "detachment, under a discreet officer, who would be advised personally before acting, in our judgement, would be a safe course." The judge concluded by stating, "I think from what I can learn that the immunity enjoyed by the deserters is producing a very bad effect; and if not checked soon, will be difficult to deal with."[19]

Forced to deal with the renegades, Finegan wrote to Brigadier General Thomas Jordan, chief of staff in Charleston:

> The deserters in question are located in the Middle District, in a large and difficult swamp on the coast, and have increased so much in number and boldness as to endanger the peace and safety of the neighborhood, and unless promptly arrested will prove demoralizing to the service. They are not confined to deserters from the troops serving in the Middle District, but are supposed to embrace many from the armies of Virginia and Tennessee. I am led to believe they have communication with the enemy on the coast, from whom they receive aid and comfort. If approved by the commanding general, I will order a discreet officer, with a sufficient number of men to prevent effectual resistance, to proceed to the section of country infested by these deserters and station them there sufficiently long to arrest the gang.[20]

State militias undertook systematic efforts to destroy the deserters. Bloodhounds were employed to track them down, but the dense swamps and jungle-like hummocks proved almost impenetrable. The dark swamps harbored millions of hiding places.

To the Union, these refugee bands were invaluable. They were the eyes and ears of the Union garrisons in Florida. The refugees kept intelligence of Confederate troop movements flowing into Union camps. They wreaked havoc on the local countryside, keeping Southerners' nerves on edge and creating a growing hostility between the citizenry and local government officials. Most importantly, the refugees provided manpower for the Federal ranks. On June 6, 1864, Union Major General John G. Foster, commanding the department of the South, commenced full scale recruiting in Florida. He was determined to enroll all white males between the ages of eighteen and fifty to be mustered in militia companies. A bounty was later offered as an added incentive.[21]

Toward the end of 1863, Yankee regulars had also infiltrated Southwest Florida. In Fort Myers, Henry A. Crane of the Second Florida Cavalry, Union, was commissioned captain on February 19, 1864. Captain Crane's company recruited fifty-one men, mostly refugees, and it was Captain Crane's job to hold the garrison and to disrupt the flow of Confederate beef.[22]

At any rate, the hordes of deserters, holdouts, and Union sympathizers occupying camps in the swamps and foraging and menacing Florida homesteaders were of grave concern to both government and soldiers who had families. Florida soldiers were loyal fighters for the Confederacy as long as protecting their own homes was part of the bargain; send them away from home and it was a very different situation. Finegan and the Sixth had their hands full.

The Sixth Florida was, of course, part of a larger military unit commanded by Brigadier General Joseph Finegan. That brigade consisted of two infantry battalions, one battalion of cavalry, plus numerous independent units of cavalry and infantry. Also included were two companies of light artillery. By December 1863, Finegan's command numbered 1,177 men present for duty, ninety-five of whom were officers. Although its numbers seemed an adequate strength to protect East Florida, the brigade desperately needed heavy cannon. During the winter of 1863, the Sixth Florida, with its varied duties, protected an area consisting of hundreds of square miles with only eight pieces of artillery to repel an enemy attack. It was always possible that the brigade would be needed outside Florida: it was, after all part of a Confederate army fighting further north.[23]

Twice Finegan's brigade was ordered to be ready to move north on a moment's notice. General P. G. T. Beauregard notified Finegan on October 22, 1863, that a Federal force had left Charleston heading southward to a "destination not known." Also on Christmas Eve, Finegan was ordered to "hold your Infantry in readiness to be sent to

Savannah, for temporary service." Later, Finegan was assured his troops would not be disturbed or "moved from their stations," as Savannah would be reinforced by troops from elsewhere. Although the Sixth Florida Battalion was on standing alert to move out quickly, by the end of the year the companies of the battalion had not yet consolidated into one large fighting force, since there was no present danger requiring such action. However, after the New Year, the circumstances long awaited crystallized as a large Union force sailed southward and disembarked at Jacksonville. The Florida expedition was about to begin and would culminate in the single major battle fought on Florida soil,[24] and the Sixth would be directly involved.

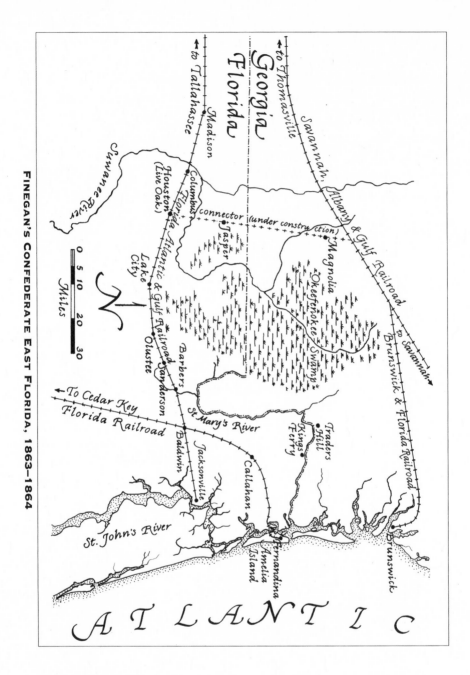

FINEGAN'S CONFEDERATE EAST FLORIDA, 1863–1864

4.

A BATTLE, REORGANIZATION AND REMOVAL

The ten companies of the Sixth Florida Battalion remained posted at their respective locations throughout January and early February 1864, performing such perfunctory duties as carrying on reconnaissance, capturing deserters, and gathering and distributing subsistence for the commissariat. During this time Federal troop movements were minimal and non-threatening.

Back in Lake City, Captain Stewart of Company E resigned his commission on January 7, and Green H. Hunter, no relation to W. A., a doctor who migrated from Georgia prior to the war, was elected captain to fill the vacancy. The Hunters, father, W. A., and recently joined son Young, meanwhile, were kept together and detached as provost guards in Lake City. They remained there until early February, when the enemy threatened Lake City.

On February 7, 1864, a substantial Federal force consisting of many Black troops steamed into the St. Johns River and occupied Jacksonville with very little resistance. The next day Camp Finegan, located eight miles west of the city, also fell into Union hands. In the frantic shuffle to evacuate the small earthen fort, numerous Confederate soldiers were captured, many of whom belonged to the Sixth Florida Battalion. Included in the list of Confederate prisoners were two officers: Captain James Eichelberger of Company K and Lieutenant Joseph Barco of Company G. The captives were sent to a Federal prison on Johnson Island, New York, via Hilton Head, South Carolina. (Barco died there the following July, but Captain Eichelberger survived the war and was paroled in June 1865.)[1]

On February 9, W. A. wrote that his company was on detail when word arrived that Camp Finegan had surrendered. Immediately Company E returned to its old camp near Lake City. "We are here now but how long we will stay I cant say we have every thing packed and ready to leave at a minutes warning. The Yankees is pushing on Baldwin." W. A. expressed concern that so few troops were left to check the enemy's advance, but remained optimistic by anticipating the arrival of 5,000 additional troops from Georgia and South Carolina within a couple of days, "Then the ball will open."[2]

When W. A. drafted this letter to his wife, Rebecca, Young was cooking his breakfast, and was in "fine spirits." However, the fine spirits were short-lived. The next day Young was ordered to report to the isolated post at Columbus Bridge on the Suwannee River thirty miles west of Lake City. From the moment of his arrival there, Young despised his new detail, writing, "It is one of the worst places I think I eaver was at I am not satisfied hear at tall in fact none of the men is satisfied hardley."[3]

Rumors of Union forces advancing from the west abounded. With equal intensity came news that the enemy was approaching from the east. The soldiers posted to guard the bridge were afraid they would be forced to cross the bridge to the west in order to halt an enemy advance on Lake City, the headquarters of East Florida. Summing up the general attitude of the soldiers, Young wrote, "A great many of them say they wont cros the River their is two or thre companys of Georgias station hear and two peases of artillery they say we have got to fortirfy the plase."[4]

Although Columbus post lived in constant fear of enemy attack, Young denied the existence of any real threat of Union advancement. "I dont believe the Yankes will eaver come hear for their is nothing for them to come for."[5]

On February 10 Confederate forces evacuated Sanderson, a small town twenty-one miles east of Lake City. The Federal force under General Truman Seymour entered in time to see three warehouses full of corn, turpentine, and resin burning to ashes. Here, Union officials also found a document drafted by the chief of commissary revealing the desperate state of the Confederate army and its "dependence on Florida for its supply of animal food."[6]

General Finegan ordered a militia unit to act as forward scouts and to report the enemy's advancing movements back to him. Often these scouts confronted the enemy in attempts to delay their swift movements, resulting in brief skirmishes. Nathan Hunter, W. A.'s nephew, belonged to one of these reconnaissance groups.

On February 10 Nathan's company was ordered to observe the enemy position and make contact through a series of dashing skirmishes to delay the rapid Federal advance. Nathan's company engaged an enemy party along the cold banks of the St. Marys River. Union numbers soon overwhelmed Nathan's outfit. Only two soldiers from his company escaped to Lake City; the remainder lay on the cold riverbank dead or badly wounded.

The battle could be heard at the Frazer Farm located nearby. After hearing the blunt popping of the muskets die away to ominous silence, the mistress of the farm took an old and trusted slave with her to inspect the scene. There she found Nathan lying on the bank, alive but bleeding profusely. The slave carried Nathan to her wagon and transported him back to the farmhouse where Mrs. Frazer doctored his wounds. Later, when the Yankees arrived in search of wounded Rebels, Mrs. Frazer hid the boy under the floorboards of her house.[7]

Three days later, news of his wounds reached his uncle, Joseph Young, who was stationed in Lake City. In a letter drafted on February 13 to his wife Arietta, Joseph stated, "Nathan Hunter is still alive. His wound is doing very well. He was hit in the side." Joseph was not aware of Mrs. Frazer's charity, for he regretfully concludes, "He is in the hands of the enemy at Barbers." Nathan's wound proved more serious than Joseph had reported. In fact, it was mortal. Mrs. Frazer's nursing proved fruitless. By nightfall Nathan had bled to death. Mrs. Frazer could not close the wound.[8]

Upon receiving the sad news concerning his son's death, John Hunter hitched a team of horses to a buckboard wagon and set off to fetch Nathan's body from Mrs. Frazer. It was a difficult journey: John was forced to circumvent the large Union force which was continually heading west. To add to his difficulty, the weather was exceedingly cold for the area and the palmetto scrub was powdered with a dusty layer of frost. John retrieved his son's body and returned home. Nathan was the first person to be buried in the Bethel Church cemetery and the first Hunter casualty of the war. John contracted a cold from the trip and was restricted to bed. The sickness lingered and soon his cold progressed into pneumonia that was eventually fatal.[9]

On the morning of the February 11, W. A. stationed at the depot in Lake City, complained that "I have cold enough to last me the balance of my life." Again he confirmed to Rebecca the state of alert by indicating his uncertainty as to how long the company would stay in Lake City. Having heard news from the "army below" that the enemy was advancing on Lake City, W. A. feared a battle would be fought "this evening or tomorrow; I think it will come off tomorrow." The two forces met sooner than that.[10]

On the eleventh, General Seymour's force edged to within three miles of Lake City. At 9:30 AM W. A. added a postscript to his letter and announced, "the fight is commenced." However, the battle proved to be only a skirmish: Seymour's uncertainty about General Finegan's troop strength forced him to retreat to Sanderson shortly after twelve o'clock noon. Joseph Young reported, "The big fight turned out to be a small skirmish. No body was hurt on our side." For his over-cautious judgment Seymour received harsh criticism following the Florida campaign[11].

Seymour's superior troop strength could have easily overwhelmed Finegan's mixed band of fifteen hundred infantry, calvalry, and artillery. However, in retreating to Barber's Plantation near Sanderson, Seymour allowed Finegan crucial time to collect a fighting force of forty-six hundred infantry and six hundred cavalry as Brigadier General Alfred H. Colquitt and his brigade of Georgia regulars arrived. Finegan scored a great tactical and moral victory.

Taking advantage of Seymour's retreat, Finegan relocated his force to Camp Beauregard near Olustee Station, thirteen miles east of Lake City. This act removed the impending battle from the streets of Lake City, and in so doing, preserved civilian life and protected personal property. The move was equally important in securing the safety of army headquarters. Most importantly, though, Finegan made the forest his front line, and he carved formidable earthen works into the ground. Seymour, having lost his chance for sudden victory, would now have to fight a substantially larger force in unfamiliar surroundings.[12]

In a letter to his wife, dated the eighteenth, Joseph Young apprized Arietta of the situation.

> We are camped on the Olustee, on the R.R. . . . The Genl is concentrating here. Genl Colquitt arrived with the most of his Brigade yesterday. They are noble looking fellows. I know them of old. Soldiered with them in Virginia. I suppose we are getting plenty of troops now & predict in a day or so you will hear of forward movement. The troops are in fine fighting order . . . Kiss our dear little Alma & all love to you dear Detta & may God bless you.[13]

Brigadier General Joseph
Finegan led Florida troops in
1862 and led the brigade in
Virginia.

A Georgia native, Brigadier
General Alfred H. Colquitt was
the field general in the Battle of
Olustee.

Brigadier General Truman
Seymour led the Northern
troops in the Olustee campaign.

Colonel John M. Martin of
Marion County, commanding
the Ninth Florida

In the early morning of February 20, Seymour concentrated his troops and moved westward toward Lake City. He followed the Florida Atlantic Gulf Central Railroad with the primary intention of capturing Lake City and continuing on to Columbus Bridge, where he felt Finegan would take his final stand. Destroying Columbus Bridge would mean the crucial Confederate communication and main transportation link with West Florida would be lost, a secondary goal for General Seymour. It was not to be. Seymour never reached the Suwannee, nor did he reach Lake City.[14]

As the Federal force neared Olustee, Finegan ordered two cavalry units under Colonel Caraway Smith to "advance and skirmish with the enemy," to draw Seymour into the strong Confederate battle lines. About noon the two forces met four miles east of Finegan's lines, and Colonel Smith fired the first shot starting the Battle of Olustee. Smith succeeded in pulling Union forces closer to Finegan, but a cautious Seymour halted two miles from Finegan's line.[15]

To reinforce Smith's cavalry, General Finegan ordered Colquitt's Brigade "out of the entrenchments" to the front. After an hour of rapid fire, the Confederates ran seriously low on ammunition. Quite some time passed before word reached the rear for much needed aid. For a period of twenty minutes during the heated battle, Confederate forces stood their ground without a single round of ammunition.[16]

To reinforce Colquitt's threatened position, Finegan made the decision to move the engagement from his predetermined battle line to the present battle site. Finegan ordered the Sixth Florida Battalion under Major Bird, along with other units, to supply Colquitt and take up battle lines. W. A. Hunter along with his battalion advanced to the battle site and witnessed a stubbornly contested fight. The Sixth Florida troops were posted on the extreme right, along the south side of the railroad tracks. There they opened deadly enfilade on the Northern Eighth Colored Corps, inflicting such severe damage as to compel them to fall back in mass confusion, abandoning five pieces of artillery in the process.[17]

Once again, ammunition ran low and the order to cease-fire and hold positions resounded along Confederate lines. A fresh supply of ammunition was brought from the ordnance wagon and distributed to the soldiers on the field.[18]

Having expended reserves, General Seymour decided to withdraw,

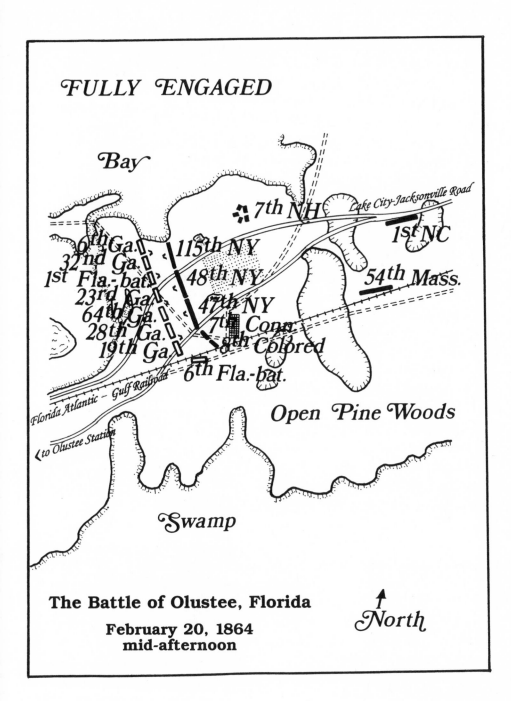

FULLY ENGAGED

Bay

Lake City-Jacksonville Road

✿ 7th NH

1st NC

6th Ga.
32nd Ga.
1st Fla.-bat.
23rd Ga.
64th Ga.
28th Ga.
19th Ga.

115th NY

48th NY

54th Mass.

47th NY

7th Conn.

8th Colored

6th Fla.-bat.

Florida Atlantic – Gulf Railroad

◁ to Olustee Station

Open Pine Woods

Swamp

The Battle of Olustee, Florida

February 20, 1864
mid-afternoon

↑
North

and by daybreak he initiated a full-scale retreat. A few days later he had returned to his point of departure, Jacksonville. The Confederates hesitated to pursue until two days later when the repair of the railroad secured supply and communication lines. By this time, the opportunity to inflict further damage on the Union force was lost.[19]

General Finegan later received sharp criticism for failing to pursue Seymour during the Union general's retreat to Jacksonville. Finegan had ordered his calvary officer, Colonel Caraway Smith, to overtake the enemy and engage him, but the order was not carried out. Finegan claimed he sent repeated dispatches to Smith, who purported to have received none. The lack of dispatch evidence supported Colonel Smith; consequently, General P.G.T. Beauregard held General Finegan responsible for allowing Seymour's shattered force to escape.[20]

Finegan's name received a second stain following the Battle of Olustee. He allowed obvious abuse of captured Black soldiers. Eyewitnesses from both sides record such brutalities as rifle butts to the head and bayoneting. Blacks were not the only unfortunate abused; the captured white officers who commanded Black troops were treated with less respect than those who led white troops. One chronicler of General Finegan's story points out that Finegan's behavior probably was a result of his plantation's being sacked by the enemy and the eager manner in which his slaves had joined in the personal destruction of his private property.[21]

Both sides suffered high casualty rates. Seymour lost 1,861 men: 203 were killed outright, 1,052 were wounded and 506 were declared missing. Finegan's camp suffered 946 casualties with 93 killed, 847 wounded and six missing. The Sixth Florida Battalion was in the thick of the fighting, exposing itself in an advanced position on the right flank, accounting for the high number of casualties. Companies C, D, F, and G appeared to see heavier fighting, as witnessed by the number of casualties in these units. In Company C four men were wounded and five men were killed outright, the highest death rate of all the companies. In Company D ten men were wounded, four of whom died later, while one was killed outright. In Company F nine men were wounded, one of whom died later, and one was killed outright. In Company G nine men were wounded, one dying later, and three of whom were killed during the battle. The total casualty list numbered eighty-two, plus two men from Company H who deserted during battle, raising the total to eighty-four men lost.[22]

W. A.'s Company E suffered only one casualty, a Private Thomas Griffin, who was "slightly wounded" during the battle. Although W. A. was not wounded in the Battle of Olustee, nor was his son, Young, directly engaged, the Hunters suffered a grave loss. W. A.'s brother-in-law Lieutenant Joseph Young of Company D was hit in the left shoulder by a Union minié ball. The bullet lodged against the bone and was removed in a Lake City hospital, and for eighteen days Joseph clung deliriously to life. As a result of his wound the left arm had to be removed. Slipping in and out of consciousness, Joseph thought of his beloved "Detta" and their sweet little Alma barely a month old. On March 9, infection overtook Joseph, and he passed away peacefully in his Lake City hospital bed.[23]

As a united fighting body, the Sixth Florida Battalion had met its first threat and succeeded in ensuring the security of eastern Florida. The Florida men were heroes. Four days after the Battle of Olustee the *Charleston Daily Courier* voiced their accolades.

All hail to our "Little Sister" Florida. The Yankees will see more the more they meddle with such men as General Joseph Finegan and his Floridians, and such Georgians and soldiers as follow Colquitt and Harrison.

The editor then charged other Confederate states to act upon Florida's aggressive example. "Will Alabama and Mississippi let Sherman plant a crop around Meridian?"[24]

Following the Battle of Olustee, the Sixth Florida Battalion was ordered to take post at Tampa. En route to Fort Brooke, they received a change in orders, and the unit repaired to Orange Springs to fend off an enemy advance up the Oklawaha River from Welaka. By March they had returned to Camp Milton, near Jacksonville, to keep a close eye on Federal forces. While at Camp Milton, the troops were commended for "performing a hard and important outpost and picket duty night and day, lying close to the enemy, and on several occasions driving them back when they were out in force, and while under cover of the fire from their gunboats and batteries."[25]

Meanwhile, Young Hunter fell prey to smallpox and was taken from his post on the Suwannee and isolated in Columbus with four others from his outfit: John Hancock, John Sapp, James Newman, and William McClennan. By mid-March, Young wrote that he was up and about and, barring any relapses, would be available for duty within two weeks. Evidently he must have felt fairly strong because he asked for, but was refused, permission to accompany Captain Hunter to Lake City. It would take until early May for Young to fully recover.[26]

W. A. found himself separated from the main body of the Sixth Florida Battalion following Olustee. He remained detached as a guard in Lake City, where morale was very low. On March 22, following a rainstorm that washed out the railroad between Lake City and Baldwin, W. A. began a letter to Rebecca by stating sardonically, "I am not drowned yet."[25] The rain had left W. A. with "wet feet" and a sickly feeling. Although W. A. was only thirteen miles from his farm, rigorous duty prevented him from visiting home frequently. He contented himself with writing. "We have two houses to guard now I have to stand 7 hours out of 24; two of our men stands 12 hours out of 24 I don't think we will put up with it verry long." Since he was unable to get home on a regular basis, W. A. resorted to managing his farm through correspondence with Rebecca.[27]

Often he instructed her on what supplies to purchase or sell or how to sow and reap crops. "I would like to have the cotton that belongs to the government packed in a little sacke and sent up." In April, during one of W. A.'s rare visits home, Rebecca confessed to him she feared salamanders were infesting the potato crops. The following day W. A. wrote, "I looked yestarday and couldent say for certain you had better have the dirt taken off the bank and then you can tell whether they are in it or not."[28]

W. A. often thought about the welfare of his slaves during the Union threat in the spring of 1864. It was his desire to keep them separated from any outside contact that might influence their leaving. W. A. instructed them to "lie out untill the Yankees are gone" and ordered Rebecca to "keep a lookout or they will be on them when you dont think abot them." W. A. owned one recalcitrant slave who continuously caused problems. W. A. instructed his wife to keep their slave Dane at home under close scrutiny, but if the Yankees entered the vicinity he also was to be allowed sanctuary in the open country.[29]

Young's illness also weighed heavily upon W. A. In a letter to Rebecca dated April 20, he wrote:

I heard from Young yesterday Eavining he is up though not

verry well two new cases of small pox yesterday there has been some three or four deaths from it my master (Leut. Largen) was as fraid of the greens as a negro would be with a red shirt.[30]

W. A. had the welfare of the remainder of his family to concern himself with also. Seventeen-year-old Calhoun was suffering from pain in the kidneys. The family physician, Dr. Hill, prescribed watermelon tea and a warm bath, and if the pain continued, to put "pepper or mustard" over the kidney area.[31]

To complicate matters, Rebecca was five months pregnant and W. A. feared for her health. He questioned her ability to manage the farming business properly while also attending to the needs of the family. Compassionately W. A. helped in managing the affairs through his letters. Moreover, he prayed that Rebecca might bear the heavy burden forced upon her.

While the Sixth Florida Battalion patrolled a triangular sector from Lake City to Orange Springs to Camp Milton near Jacksonville, W. A. remained stationary in Lake City. Many of the Confederate troops who had fought at Olustee had left the state. W. A. felt he was going to stay near home. On April 20, he wrote:

> I dont think there is any danger of being sent off soon; all the troops except the Ga Regulars (Colquitts Brigade] & some Ga Cavalry and the Fla troops is sent off so I think our chance verry good to stay here for some time yet.[32]

However, W. A. was not aware of plans being formulated in the Confederate Capital to organize three additional infantry regiments from Florida. This reorganization plan became fact on April 28, 1864, when Special Order Number Ninety-nine renamed the Sixth Florida Battalion the Ninth Florida Infantry, C.S.A. The odd-designator of "battalion" would now be dropped and the more recognizable appellation "regiment" would identify the group of unified companies. The Ninth was one of three new regiments organized at this time: orders were also given to create the Tenth and Eleventh Infantry Regiments.[33]

In March Major General Patton Anderson took a new post as commander of the districts of East and West Florida. On May 16 General Anderson received an order from Adjutant and Inspector General Samuel Cooper to consolidate all available troops, including the three newly formed regiments, into one brigade under Brigadier General Joseph Finegan and send all troops "with greatest possible expedition" to Richmond. Anderson complied promptly with the order, informing Richmond the following day that he was sending a brigade to Virginia. However, concern for the safety of the state forced him to "leave one regiment in the district and two battalions of cavalry, 3 companies of artillery, one siege and two light artilleries. There will remain also, 1 Brigadier General and 3 Colonels." One reason Anderson left troops in Florida was to protect the flow of Florida beef to Virginia.[34]

On the morning of May 18, the ten companies of the new Ninth Regiment pulled up stakes and headed north. That evening the companies converged at Madison, Florida, and some time after seven o'clock shouldered their baggage and marched twelve miles, crossing the Georgia border. W. A. was at home when he received the order to move out. The parting was extremely painful for the dutiful W. A. He adored his wife and children and fully expected he would never see their bright faces again. Indeed, W. A. wondered if he would survive to see the child growing in Rebecca's womb. The pain of leaving his family, the weight of responsibility forced upon Rebecca, the need to look out for Young's welfare, and the reality of the war burdened W. A. After many tearful hugs and kisses W. A. and Young made haste for Lake City to join their company.[35]

W. A. left Lake City at eight in the morning on May 18, with the Ninth Florida, and reached Madison shortly after seven in the evening, "Just in time to march [with] my company." He mentioned an additional twelve-mile hike which ended when they finally camped, "tired down and a little wet," because it rained on the expedition. W. A. slept soundly that night.[36]

When the sun rose the following morning, the Ninth Florida, with a total muster of 1,289 men, saw 656 men, a little over half of the enrollment, break camp and head north on an arduous, seven-day journey to Richmond.[37] They were leaving territory from which most of them had never strayed, homes dependent on them for safety from the wild foraging of the swamp deserters. They were joining a cause that was more than half broken, and to which they were not closely allied. It would not be a comfortable trip.

After a late start, the regiment marched thirteen miles to the Savannah and Gulf Railroad terminal located in Quitman, Georgia. They arrived shortly after four o'clock in the afternoon, then boarding a transport train around five o'clock for Savannah. Traveling through the night, the Hunters arrived in Savannah around five o'clock the following morning. Shortly after arrival, the Florida soldiers were ushered into another train that immediately set out for Charleston, South Carolina, arriving at eight o'clock the evening of May 20.[38]

By the time the Florida brigade reached Charleston, spirits had begun to ebb. Hunger, exhaustion, and realization that orders to the battlefront in Virginia were imminent, sobered the unit. W. A. wrote:

> I am in Charleston to night we leave at six in the morning for Virginia we never knew where we was a goin untill we got here to knight then we were told we had to go to VA . . . We are cooking up two days rashions to knight. I suppose you would like to hear how I stood the trip all I can say was did make out to keep up but I will assure you that it was all that I could do if we hadent got through as soon as we did I would a give out I feel rested some to knight but wont get to sleep mutch to knight; Young complained of being verry tyrard we are both well in body but sick in mind.[39]

Whatever their own personal reservations, the Florida soldiers were heroes in the adoring eyes of the Charleston residents. As the Ninth Regiment marched through the city streets they "were chased all the way by the ladys in Charleston it was deafning the boys kept sutch hollering."

The cheers did little to allay the greatest fear among the Florida force headed to Virginia. Their worry focused on the Yankee threat they had left behind. Who would protect their homes and families now that most troops were being sent north? W. A. asked Rebecca:

> Dont you think the Yanks will go all oaver East Fla if all the troups is taken away you must do like your neighbors I want you to do the best with the children you can if the Yankees will let you alone.[40]

Not despairing, W. A. closed his letter to Rebecca.

I don't expect to be back soon if ever; kiss Bell & Rhett & Estele for me tell Calhoun & John & Hayan howdy and Malissa & Sue is old enuff to know how to do Malissa do that that is wright I never expect to see you again so fare well Rebecca try and bear up as well as you can the Lord will provide for you if you will put your trust in him; do at this time take care of your self and all the children it is now ten o clock; Farwell if we never meet in this life I hope to met in heaven[41]

At six AM of the twenty-first, the Ninth Florida left Charleston for Richmond. Later that same day the transport halted at Fair Bluff, North Carolina, where the regiment awaited a transfer of cars. They were scheduled to depart the following morning at 9:00 o'clock.[42]

After spending a restless night at the depot, W. A. recorded his general feelings and fears.

We will leave here at nine this morning for Wilmington and then we go to Petersburg and I dont know where we will stop but we are certain to go where the fighting is going on. Dear wife I and Young is well but I am low in spirits we have got on verry well so far Except being stop at this time I hear that they are fighting in VA we are busing on to the conflict I am living on hard bread and meat you may be sure that I dont eate mutch of it I feel better today and yesterday than I had felt for some days my bowels has got in better fix; the men is all well that went from your settlement . . . we are in a verry poore country you now that without me telling you children I want to do as well as you can and help your mother If the Yankees come in the country I want you to do as your neighbors do Rebecca try and take care of our children and be sure and take the best care of yourself that you can for there is verry heavy responcibillity resting on you more than you can bear I fear. Kiss all the babys for me and tell all the children & Blacks howdy for me . . . farewell if we meet no more in this life I hope to meet you where troubel is not nowing.[43]

Not all the Florida troops were depressed. Youthful Young was enthusiastic and enjoyed "him self as well as the circumstances permitted."[44]

The next stop along the road to Richmond was Wilmington, North Carolina. Here the Florida soldiers halted for a brief interlude, then continued on their odyssey at 10:30 PM of the twenty-second. Their train traveled through the night and arrived in Petersburg, Virginia, on May 24. North of Petersburg the train halted at the southern end of a five-mile section of track torn up by the enemy. Forced out of the cars, the travel-weary regiment walked the remaining fourteen miles to Richmond. During the march, the Ninth passed fresh graves marking the scene of battle the previous week when General Beauregard "whipped" a Federal force under General Benjamin Butler, driving the "Beast" back to his gunboats.[45]

At approximately 11:30 in the morning of May 25, the new Ninth Florida Regiment rested on the "green" of the Capitol Square in Richmond awaiting their orders. The Tenth and Eleventh Regiments would arrive at a later date. W. A. took the opportunity to draft a letter to Rebecca describing his condition.

> I & Young is well we have stood the trip tollerable well considering all things my bowels is still derange but not so bad but I can go with my company . . . I will say this mutch that we havent any meat to eat now havent Drawn any since we left Charleston I have had some to eat evryday and has Enuff for one more meal we will get some to morrow or they tell us so . . . P.S. We will leave here as soon as we can draw rashines I dont know where but I supose we go to Lees army he is fighting and falling back at this time; dont grieve for me and Young the Lords will be done; Young looks rather low spirited this morning.[46]

The answer came promptly. Shortly after noon, the Ninth Florida Regiment was ordered to proceed immediately by rail to Hanover Junction. There they were ordered to join General Robert. E. Lee's Army of Northern Virginia near the banks of the South Anna River for assignment to active duty. In less than three days, the Hunters and the Ninth Regiment would arrive at the "real war."[47]

5.

A TASTE OF GLORY

In the spring of 1864, General Ulysses S. Grant drove his army of 113,000 across the Potomac southward into Virginia intent on capturing Richmond, the Confederate capital, and putting an end to the long war. General Robert E. Lee's Army of Northern Virginia, numbering 62,000, positioned itself between the enemy and Richmond to thwart that goal. On May 5 the two armies met near Fredericksburg and clashed in a thickly wooded area called the Wilderness. The savage battle was fought at point-blank range. Flames emitting from cannon and musket fire set the woods ablaze, burning alive many helpless wounded.

Grant found Lee deeply entrenched in the Wilderness, so by May 7 Grant turned his attention to Spotsylvania. The two armies clashed again on May 12 at Spotsylvania Courthouse.

Again, Grant was checked and forced to formulate new plans for his assault on Richmond. He moved his men south to the North Anna River, a short distance north of Hanover Junction. Lee, anticipating Grant's next move, remained an obstacle blocking the path to Richmond. By May 25 both sides were entrenched along the banks of the North Anna: Grant's army, strong and massive; Lee's army, dwindling and in dire need of fresh reinforcements. Fortunately for the Southern general, some relief, in the form of a fresh but reluctant Florida brigade, would arrive within twenty-four hours.

On May 26 after nine days on the road, the Ninth Florida arrived at Lee's headquarters near Hanover Junction, twenty-four miles north of Richmond. The brigade was bone-weary with a great many of the men too tired to cook their meat. They satisfied themselves by eating it raw. W. A. wrote we have "been nine days on the road we traveled day and night except two nights so you can tell how we feel."[1]

The Ninth Regiment was not immediately aware of the command to which it would be assigned. In fact, they were not ever aware that they were now the Ninth Regiment. Uninformed of the restructuring which had occurred in April, enlisted men thought they still belonged to the Sixth Florida Battalion. The new Florida regiment was assigned to General Richard Anderson's division of A. P. Hill's Corps. Major General Anderson himself was absent, after having been wounded during the Battle of the Wilderness. His command was temporarily passed on to William Mahone, a short, fastidious, intense thirty-seven-year-old brigadier general from Southern Virginia.[2]

In a letter to Rebecca dated May 26, 1864, W. A. admitted that he expected to be in the center of the fight soon.

> The firing is going on we look Every minuet for orders to the front they been skirmishing here for the las three days we hold our position and the Yankees is trying to drive us out . . . I dont no when the Drum will beat for us to fall in.[3]

In closing, W. A. urged his wife to give herself no "uneasyness . . . we will do the best we can and trust on the Lord for help I hope we will be spared."[4]

Although the new Florida regiments arrived in Virginia on May 25, they were without the services of their leader, General Finegan, until his arrival on May 28. The same day the new Ninth, Tenth, and Eleventh regiments were consolidated with the remnants of the veteran Second, Fifth, and Eighth Florida Infantry regiments under the command of Brigadier General Edward A. Perry. These war-weary veterans from Florida had been serving in Virginia since 1862.[5]

Later that day the Hunters were placed in the line of battle fully expecting to fight by nightfall. However, only light skirmishing ensued before the darkness of night fell. Grant took full advantage of the darkness and removed his troops from the area. Once again revising his plan, Grant now followed the Pamunkey River downstream to Hanovertown, skirting Lee in an attempt to flank the Confederates and capture Richmond.

By May 29 Finegan's brigade was entrenched nine miles west of Richmond in a battle line four miles west of Atlee's station on the Virginia Central Railroad line.[6]

The weather had been very warm and rainy up to the morning of the twenty-ninth when it turned "quite cool." The Florida brigade marched "pretty hard" to remain between Grant and Richmond. W. A. expressed his dislike of Virginia and complained that it had rained "some little every day since we left home." However, he admitted the wet weather has been an advantage to the mobile troops, as it held down the dust considerably.[7]

Aside from the climate, other external forces added to the difficulty of soldiering in Virginia. Being new arrivals, many of the men carried extra gear brought from home. W. A. wrote:

> My Baggage is two heavy I will be Compelled to throw Some of my things away I am at a loss to know what to throw away; I will have to quit my under shirt how I will do without it I cant tell but I will have to do the best I can[8]

Two days later the Confederates were deeply entrenched in a line from the Virginia Central Railroad one mile north of Atlee's station to the Chickahominy River fifteen miles to the south. During the two-day interim, Finegan had ordered his troops to entrench. W. A. stated, "we have a hard time we work on batterys." Expectations of enemy attack were a daily event and picket fighting was constant around the Florida brigade. On the May 30 a heavy cannonading erupted near Finegan's breastworks. "Shells fell near me I hear them whistle and burst in a few hundred yards of us," wrote W. A.[9]

The soldiers contended not only with picket fire and cannon blasts, but also with harsh environmental and working conditions. These factors began to adversely affect the Floridians. "I am verry dirty I have no time to clean my self; I stand it very well considering what we have to do My throat is quite sore this morning but hope not serious."[10]

On the afternoon of June 1, Mahone called his division into battle formation in an attempt to push a portion of the Federal invasion force across to the north side of the Totopotomoy River. In a brief encounter Mahone succeeded in capturing 150 Union prisoners. Once the Federal troops disappeared from Mahone's front, Lee ordered the division to reposition itself on the far right of the line. Battling choking clouds of dust, scorching heat, and piercing thirst, the Florida brigade marched to Turkey Hill, also called Turkey Ridge, near the Chickahominy River on June 2. There the brigade positioned itself to support General John C. Breckenridge's troops.[11]

Shortly after the brigade's arrival, a Union cavalry squadron under General Philip Sheridan advanced through an open field one-half a mile wide toward Breckenridge and Finegan. Confederate artillery checked the enemy's advance, preventing heavy loss of life to both sides. However, the Ninth Florida Regiment received two casualties. Both men were members of Samuel Hope's Company C. Charles Anderson was severely wounded and died in a Richmond hospital on June 10, 1864. William H. Allen, also wounded, was admitted to Petersburg General Hospital. To complicate his wound, Allen also suffered from acute diarrhea, a common ailment, and he contracted typhoid fever. All this proved too much for Private Allen, and he died in the hospital June 27. These men were the first casualties of the Ninth Florida in Virginia.[12]

Following the skirmish of Turkey Ridge, Finegan's brigade fell into reserve ranks behind Breckenridge, who was situated between the brigades of Wilcox and Hoke. There the men rested, undoubtedly excited from their initial taste of battle, and interested in seeing what the new morning would bring.[13] What it brought was Cold Harbor.

As dawn broke on the morning of June 3, the Florida brigade awoke early, fearing an imminent attack. At approximately 4:30 AM Grant launched a massive assault covering a six-mile front. Thousands of Union troops rushed across open ground between the two lines. Grant's plan was to drive his stiff, compact columns into Lee's protected ranks, crushing them. However, superior Confederate placement quickly repelled the assault with heavy losses to Grant.

Along one swampy front the Federals succeeded in penetrating Rebel lines belonging to Anderson's division. The Federal attackers emerged from a quagmire and with a furious rush broke through Breckenridge's forward line capturing a portion of the soldiers posted there. Three large field pieces were also secured in the melee and were about to be turned on the Confederates when General Finegan rushed his brigade into the breach.[14]

The Florida brigade raced toward the collapsed section of line and quickly overwhelmed the enemy forces there, recapturing the guns and inflicting severe losses on the Federals.[15]

Later in the afternoon Generals Finegan and Breckenridge advanced to establish their skirmish lines. In an effort to check this move, Federal troops met them and a heated fight ensued. During the battle General Breckenridge's horse was struck and killed by a cannon blast. The general received a deep bruise in the fall preventing him from remounting for several days. By nightfall the firing ceased along the lines. So ended the Battle of Cold Harbor, June 3, 1864.[16]

One Florida historian recorded, "at the Second Battle of Cold Harbor General Finegan and his Florida Brigade had a good opportunity for distinction, and made memorable use of the occasion to the credit of themselves and their state." The valor and fighting spirit of the new Florida regiments were unanimously applauded by the veteran troops of Perry's old brigade. Colonel R. B. Thomas, a veteran soldier, wrote in a congratulatory letter, "The new troops have shown that they are worthy compatriots of the veterans from the same state."[17]

General Finegan, however, received sharp criticism later for his actions during the Battle of Cold Harbor. He was criticized for impetuosity. When Finegan was ordered into the breach, he reestablished the Confederate line, securing the break in Breckenridge's line. However, he failed to drive the Union forces back to their original entrenchment. Compounding this error Finegan followed up with another costly mistake. He ordered two suicidal skirmish line assaults which gained him no ground and failed to push back his enemy, yet these battles cost him the lives of two valuable officers: Major Pickens B. Bird of the Ninth Regiment and the young and promising Captain C. Seton Fleming of the Second Regiment.[18]

Although the new Florida troops were heroes in the eyes of present and future comrades, to many soldiers, such as W. A., the battle was horrifying reality far more than romantic triumph. In a long letter drafted Sunday, June 5, two days after the terrible battle, W. A. painted a vivid picture of the preceding three days.

I seat my self in the trenches to let you know that I and Young is still among the living We have run some narrow Escapes but by the help of the Allmighty we have come clear so far; a shell Bursted in the trench yesterday in five feet of Young and some twenty feet of me . . . we have been two days and knights in the front this morning we were taken to the reare but we are compelled to lie in the entrenchments; on friday morning the Yanks charged our front lines and taken possession of them they were defended by some Virginia Troops; we were ordered to leave Everry thing and charge them in turn we made the charge and drove them out and killed some hundred or two since then they charged us some two or three times but we drove them back Everry time; In the fight we lost five but the Sharpe Shooters kill our men; if you raise your head in a minute you have a hole in your head; Captain Hunter was wounded Maj Bird of our Battalion is severely wounded; Captain Reynolds killed and a great many more that you would not know; today the fight is going on the same it has for the last two days nor I cant say when it will be over with but I hope it will be over with in the course of a few days; I have lost my knapsack and haversack and Everry thing I had I havent got nothing but one Blanket and the suit of clothes that I wore from home I feel verry bad and dirty Young has lost his but he put on some clothes since he left home; I am in hopes that we will do the best we can; I have been two days and knights without water or any thing to Eate but we have Plenty to Eate to day and could sleep some if we had room but we ar crouded in a ditch and no chance to sleep I feel verry bad I have a severe coughf and soreness on my breast Our company has a great many sick I dont think we have more than about forty or fifty fit for duty since the fight I cant tell how many was killed and wounded in our company you will hear by the papers as soon as I will know Rebecca I must say to you that it is a hard life and no telling when one may be killed but I cant say it was any worse than I expected it I dont think I can stand it verry long but I hope and trust the Allmighty will protect me and Young . . . do the best you can to our children I want you to send them to school as soon as you can if you cant find no teacher you can let Sue teach them . . . I want you to kiss my little ones and tell all the rest howdy for me I hope I may be spared to meet you all again but if we meet no more in this life I hope we may meet where there is no more pain nor sorrow nor death in the land where all is peace; fare well my wife and children I hope to meet you all in heaven[19]

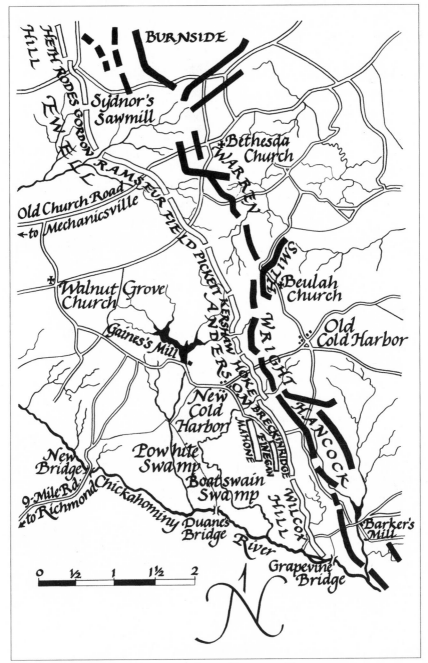

THE BATTLE OF COLD HARBOR, VIRGINIA
FRIDAY, JUNE 3, 1864 — 5:30 A.M. POSITIONS

Major General William Mahone, "the hero of the crater," led the counter-attack.

Colonel David Lang commanded the 8th Florida Regiment, part of Finegan's brigade in 1864.

Valentine Museum, Richmond

On Sunday, the men were sent to the rear for a badly needed respite, but their rest was short lived. W. A. stated, "I learn we have to go out to knight to some point I dont know where but I supose we have to fight untill we drive the Yankees away."[20]

The Battle of Cold Harbor exacted a heavy toll upon the Ninth Florida Regiment. The total count came to fifty casualties. Of these fifty, twenty-one were killed during battle, eighteen were wounded and survived, and another ten were wounded but died later. James Wimberly of Company B was declared missing in action during the battle. Companies H and E suffered the heaviest losses, reporting nine and eight casualties respectively. Quite the opposite was reported for Company C, who the day before had suffered the only casualties from the skirmish at Turkey Ridge: at Cold Harbor, Company C survived without a single casualty.[21]

Listed among the number of Ninth Regiment casualties were six invaluable officers. Regimental Major Bird was seriously wounded and admitted to Howard's Grove Hospital in Richmond the following day. There he died, but the records show two death dates: first, June 5, 1864, and second, June 6, 1864 from "vulnus sclopeticum thigh." The major died June 5 and was recorded as interred in section X, grave number 150 of Hollywood Cemetery on June 5, 1864.[22]

Regimental Adjutant James O. Owens was killed during the battle, as was Captain Benjamin L. Reynolds of Company H. Second Lieutenant Benjamin B. Lane of Company A was wounded and sent to Howard's Grove Hospital where he was admitted June 4. He was diagnosed as having "vulnus sclopeticum: both hips." He succumbed to his wounds on June 18, 1864.[23]

First Lieutenant Robert D. Harrison was also wounded and admitted to Howard's Grove on June 4. He survived and was furloughed June 22, 1864. He later returned to duty and remained with his company until the surrender at Appomattox.[24]

Second Lieutenant James Tucker of Company D, shot in the thigh, was sent to Howard's Grove Hospital on June 4. There, he recovered from his wounds, spending fourteen weeks on crutches, and on June 9, the twenty-four-year-old was appointed captain. On July 5, 1864, Tucker was furloughed for sixty days to his home in Florida. He never returned to duty and was paroled in Madison, Florida, May 16, 1865.[25]

General Finegan also received a slight wound during the battle. It was not extensive, and he continued his daily duty. If it had been serious, undoubtedly W. A. would have mentioned the general's wounds.[26]

In the days following the great battle, the Florida troops had ample opportunity to rest. On June 6, Finegan's brigade was relieved from picket by Wright's brigade of Georgia troops. Moving to the rear the men rested until called to the next twenty-four-hour watch. It was the Florida brigade's duty to hold a key position on Turkey Ridge against Union assault. Colonel David Lang of the Eighth Florida noted that although the troops were resting, the continual "popping of musketry and the occasional boom of a cannon reminds us that Grant the Giant still keeps up the cry Fe Fo Fum etc. though blood enough he has already had God knows. What blood has been shed since his On to Richmond would float a man of war." The colonel stated that the "Majic influence of old rye" was the only reason the Federal troops continued with their feeble attacks. He predicted the Yankee soldiers would soon refuse to follow such inept leadership.[27]

The days passed with little else erupting but small fire and minor skirmishes. As dawn broke on the thirteenth, the Ninth Florida awoke that peaceful Monday morning to discover Grant's "Grand Army" had slipped away during the course of the night. The Confederate camps were puzzled as to their enemy's whereabouts. Young expressed the popular sentiment when he wrote, "I believe the Yankees are gone frome hear but I dont no wheare they are gone to."[28]

Immediately the brigade was ordered to march. Skirting Richmond to the east, the troops left Turkey Ridge and reached Frazer's Farm, two miles from Malvern Hill June 16. While at Frazer's Farm the soldiers rested and drew rations.

W. A. took advantage of the occasion to eat a decent dinner and later pen a letter to Rebecca. He informed her of their position along the dusty road to Richmond and intimated his fullest expectations of crossing the James River and advancing south to Petersburg. On June 2, W. A.'s brother John C. died from the pneumonia he had contracted in February following the death of his own son, Nathan. Reflecting on the news of his brother's death, W. A. expressed regret, but he expressed deeper regrets over the death of his eldest daughter's colt. Young, feeling the grave loss of a relative, wrote, "I was sorry to hear that Uncle John was dead." W. A.'s health and that of his son were not good in the fetid swamps far, far from home.[29]

> Young is not well he has Diarhea I have a verry sore throat I trust the Lord will provide for us If we don't get help from him there is none to be had from our Doctor I don't think he know mutch and cares less; I have never reported on the sick list since I left home and I hope I never will young reported one night and was told he would be all right by morning it has been some ten or twelve days and he is not wright and I am fearful he wont get well soon . . .[30]

Their rest was short-lived, because later that same day W. A. was instructed to be ready to march in ten minutes. "I must close for the troops is moving I supose there has been several thousands passed by since I sat down to write."[31]

The following morning W. A. and the Florida brigade were camped at Chafin's Bluff a half-mile north of the James and a few miles downriver from Drewry's Bluff. "I think we are stop to watch the Yankees I think in a day or two we will be on the south side of the James River." They remained at Chafin's Bluff only briefly.[32]

Once again they took to the road. By afternoon Finegan had marched his troops toward the pontoon bridge spanning the James above Drewry's Bluff. Finegan was ordered to wait there until midnight, then cross over. It was not until three AM that the brigade followed Kershaw's division of 21,000 men over the bridge. Later that day, June 18, they passed through Petersburg and were cheered on by appreciative townspeople.[33]

By five o'clock in the evening Finegan's brigade arrived along the Petersburg entrenchment, but it was not until midnight that it arrived at its designated line of duty. Along the route to Petersburg the Florida troops witnessed a stricken countryside served by tangled rail lines. However, spirits were uplifted somewhat by the sight of Confederate troops amassed around Petersburg. "I supose there is fifty thousand around here; I Expect we will have a fight here the guns is in a continual roar I think we will give them a whipping here." Regardless of how high-spirited the soldiers tried to be, fear of death weighed heavily on their hearts, "I Expect we will have a fight here . . . there will be many a good man that will be killed the Lord only knows who will come out safe. I will let you know and if we fall I hope the Lord will take our souls to heaven."[34]

Evidently the realistic Rebecca had requested direction from W. A. in the event of his demise.

> You wanted to know who should manage your afairs if I was to be killed or die; all I can say is to name some of the men that is lef behind unless you were to do it your self If you could get some one to help you might do it your self; Your Brother James or Dr Parcks or Wm Hagin or A Miot or Capt Roberts or some sutch men as them be sure you employ an honest man; I think you had better keep as mutch of the property to gether as you can untill the children is raised or get larger; you can keep the negroes and nearly every thing by paying the dets whitch you know will be easy to pay at this time and I hope will be light at the last I cant say who because I don't know who would be willing to do it do the best you can and try to bring up the children in a wright maner I would make a will but I want what I have to be equally divided between my children after you get your portion and I hope you will be of the same oppinion; I don't know what the laws of Florida allows a woman but I think the laws better than a will unless I should want to give you more than the laws would allow them; Rebecca I may never write to you again but I trust that by the help of the Lord you will do the best you can I want you to pray for me and young and not grieve for us; the Lords will be done.[35]

The first days along the Petersburg front were spent adjusting to their new surroundings. Much of the work duty went into the construction of formidable trenches and earthen forts. W. A. took advantage of spare moments to draft long letters to Rebecca describing life in the dirty trenches. He kept her abreast of the latest news concerning the war. He always assured her that Young was fine, and that he could keep an eye on all friends since, "all the Florida Troops be longs to the same Brigade and we are close to gether all the time." The small contingent supporting the Confederacy from homes such a long distance away at least had the comfort of comradeship of fellows from home on the battle front. On numerous occasions W. A. requested from Rebecca such items as cloth, needles, thread, socks, and after Cold Harbor, a Bible.[36]

W. A. loved his son and was genuinely concerned for his well being. Young Hunter was not a fighting man as his father admits to Rebecca in a letter dated June 16, 1864. "Young appears to know what danger he is in he is the peacibles boy that we have in our company and I hope and pray that he will make his peace with his maker." Young admitted to his aversion to fighting.

> They fight some wheare on the lines eavery day but they don't call it any thing but skirmishing I was in a fight on the third and fourth of this month I hope I may neaver get in to another I lost eavery thing I had[37]

Expecting the worst during his campaign in Virginia, W. A. also desired peace with his Maker.

> I pray by the help of the Allmighty God to make my peace and reach the place where there will be no more trouble nor sorrow; I hope to meet you and my children in heaven so fare well to we meet; If we meet no more on earth I hope to meet you all in heaven;[38]

In a letter to Rebecca, drafted June 17, 1864, W. A. stressed the importance of educating his children.

> I think if you can spare Susannah she had better teach the children unless you have a school handy she can teach in the house on my place or in the house with you; I want the boys to go every chance you can send them;[39]

From the twenty-second until the end of June, the Ninth Florida joined in numerous defense engagements along the Railroad south of Petersburg. The Weldon line was a major supply route from the Deep South. It was imperative that Lee keep the Weldon open. The men of the Ninth Regiment found themselves marching day and night between their Petersburg line and Ream's Station along the Weldon line. On the twenty-second a Federal cavalry raiding party led by Brigadier General James H. Wilson clashed head-on with Mahone's division, including the Florida Ninth, at Ream's Station south of Petersburg. A fight erupted, and Mahone ordered his division into a gap between two Union corps, resulting in a swift Confederate victory. The Federals, confused and beaten, withdrew at dusk leaving in their wake sixteen hundred prisoners, four guns and eight regimental flags. In this battle, Finegan's brigade suffered a loss of sixteen men captured. It proved a small loss when compared to the monumental victory of regaining the supply line.[40]

On June 25 Wilson sallied his cavalry troops around the Weldon Railroad. W. A. hastened to complete a letter before receiving orders to pack up. And again the Florida soldiers found themselves at Ream's Station on June 29, as General Wilson threatened the railroad. Wade Hampton's cavalry pressed on Wilson's heels, driving him straight into the teeth of Mahone's division lying in wait at Ream's Station. When Wilson arrived, the Confederate division met him head-on and crushed the Union forces. The Federal casualties were extremely heavy: one thousand prisoners, thirteen hundred Negroes, and thirteen guns. However, in this victory the South also suffered a telling setback. The Federal force had succeeded in destroying approximately sixty miles of track along the Weldon line. Lee would be forced to ship his supplies by wagon train from Stony Point to Petersburg.[41]

Although the campaigns around Ream's Station between June 24 and 29 were fought fiercely at times, the Ninth Regiment suffered only six casualties. Two men were killed in the battle fought on the twenty-ninth: Sergeant W. P. Roberts of Company E and twenty-nine-year-old Second Lieutenant David L. White of Company I.[42]

Two men were wounded. Charles M. Brown, second lieutenant from Company G, was wounded in a skirmish on June 27. He was sent to Howard's Grove Hospital in Richmond July 11 and furloughed twelve days later. Private John W. Marston, also of Company G, was wounded during the engagement on the 29th. He was sent to Howard's Grove July 1, and furloughed for sixty days July 31. He went absent without leave October 31 and was captured later in Savannah sometime between December 18 and 21. He was imprisoned at Point Lookout Maryland and exchanged on February 13, 1865.[43]

Two men were also declared missing in action. Robert G. McEwen of Company B was missing following the June 24 campaign and declared captured by the Federals. He was later sent to Point Lookout prison, then transferred to Aiken's Landing Virginia, where he was exchanged March 14, 1865. He was admitted to Howard's Grove Hospital March 17, with "scrobutus." Finally, Private James R. Williams of Company K was also declared missing in action and no further reports, Confederate or Union, exist revealing his destiny.[44]

W. A. described the danger his company was in during a march to Ream's Station.

> The Yankees were shelling us we were in the open place how we were not killed I don't know unless the Allmighty saved us whitch we know was the cause; I cant discribe the scene but I hope and trust I never may see sutch a sight[45]

The second great Federal retreat from Ream's Station marked an end to the Florida Ninth Regiment's first month in Virginia. In that short time they had been incorporated into a large brigade, marched well over one-hundred miles, dug numerous trenches, built many breastworks, and fought in three heated battles where they witnessed suffering of friends and relatives. The Ninth Florida Regiment, once fresh, had begun to grow hungry, weary, and sickly. During July the war of attrition would exact its toll on the men, causing morale to plummet. Grumbling and discontent were beginning to spread through the trenches like an infectious disease, manifesting themselves in depressed spirits. Worse was yet to come.

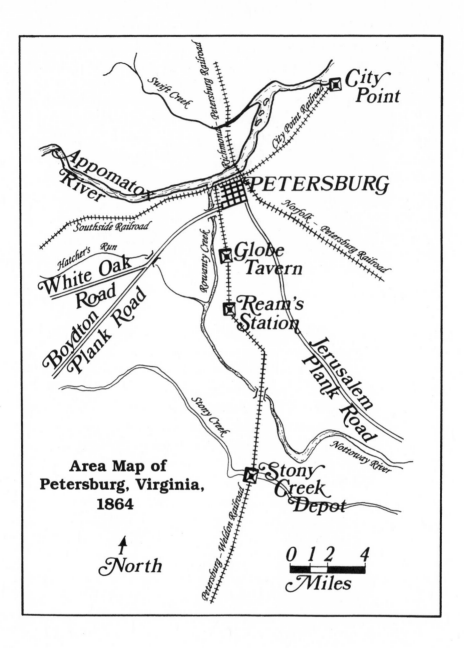

Swift Creek

Richmond & Petersburg Railroad

City Point

City Point Railroad

Appomatox River

PETERSBURG

Southside Railroad

Norfolk – Petersburg Railroad

Hatcher's Run

White Oak Road

Rowanty Creek

Globe Tavern

Boydton Plank Road

Ream's Station

Jerusalem Plank Road

Stony Creek

Nottoway River

Area Map of Petersburg, Virginia, 1864

Stony Creek Depot

Petersburg – Weldon Railroad

↑ North

0 1 2 4 Miles

6.

GLORY FADING

Following the military action along the Weldon Railroad in June, the Ninth Regiment settled down to a trench-centered war of attrition. Wilson's unsuccessful foray along the Weldon line ended all immediate hopes of Federal seizure of that section of track. The dust of marching settled as the regiment lodged itself within the safety of its breastworks. Except for occasional mortar fire or a small skirmish, affairs remained relatively quiet in the camp of the Florida brigade. The Florida soldiers began to size up their fortunes, and what they saw was plainly dissatisfying.

By mid-month absenteeism without leave increased and many men began to desert. Insufferable hardships: sickness and disease, an unfriendly climate, hunger, high prices, unpredictable pay, fatigue endured during lengthy marches, never-ending work details, tedious inspections, concerns for home and the safety of one's family, fear of the enemy, raging rumors, and poor treatment led to radical action. Subtly, also, the realization that the cause wasn't going well surfaced, and that did not add to the soldiers' enthusiasm.

The Ninth Regiment, part of Finegan's brigade, numbered 656 men upon its arrival in Richmond on May 25. By September the regiment had been reduced by two-thirds. The foreign climate and multiple hardships, disease and sickness took their toll, accounting for the largest number of absentees. Of the total men who accompanied Finegan north, 422 were admitted to a hospital at one time or another while serving in Virginia. This constituted an alarming sixty-four percent of the total regiment.[1]

The prevailing disease in camp was dysentery. W. A. Hunter began many letters to his wife complaining that both he and their son were suffering from the "bowel complaint." W. A. wrote that Young reported to the sick call August 5 and was told he would be better in the morning, but that was not the case. W. A. admitted that he was fine, "except for eating too much green corn and that upsets my constitution." On June 16, only three weeks after arriving in Virginia,

W. A. wrote, "there is a great many men that have Diarhea and I am fearful it will run in to typhoid fever." One month later he again wrote, "The prevailing Disease in Camp is Diarhea nearly all of our company is sick with it there is beginning to be some Typhoid fever I am fearful that it will prevail to some extent." Other sicknesses paralyzed the brigade also. W. A. complained of colds, coughs, sore throats, soreness in his breast, and sore eyes. The most common serious diseases in camp were typhoid fever, intermittent fever, and measles, all of which exacted a heavy death toll.[2]

Surely compounding the trouble was the unusual militia-like makeup of the original units. Older men and boys less than conscription age had helped swell the ranks, but these old men and young boys were more vulnerable to sickness than the usual robust teenager in the army.

By the end of June, the prevalence of sickness and subsequent reduction in the ranks was growing quite noticeable. On the June 27, W. A. wrote, "I will let you know how fast our Battalion is geting sick and dieing we left Florida with 500 men [W. A.'s estimate] now we cant get 200 men that is able to do duty I hope they will get better and come in." The same day Young paralleled his father's observation: "I have saw nearly all of the Florida boys thos last Florida Troopes that came on is agetting sick very fast we have ten or fifteen from our company now."[3]

By mid-July W. A. submitted to the inevitable by flatly stating, "it seems like we will all be sick in a few more weeks. Our new company is suffering at a fearful rate." Doctors offered little help in alleviating their desperate situation. "Dr. Griffin is gone to the hospital he has done no service since he come here I think he will grant out a discharge or some other bombproof position as all sutch is getting out of the way of bullets." The sick were sent to the dreaded brigade hospital. W. A. writes with vehemence when he refers to it.[4]

> We have to be nearly dead before they will take one to the hospital and then he is taken to the Brigade hospital it is some tents no place to lie Except on the ground and no one to cook or give one a drink of water there they have to stay untill they think they are nearly dead then they send them to Richmond to finish there Existence.[5]

One man in Virginia cared deeply for the plight of the suffering soldiers from Florida. He was Thomas Martin Palmer, a stalwart, bushy-bearded man, who served as surgeon-in-charge of the Florida ward of Howard's Grove Hospital in Richmond. Dr. Palmer was a native Floridian, born into a long line of doctors raised in Monticello. If you were a Palmer from Monticello, Florida, you were a doctor. Dr. Palmer watched with intense interest the high number of Florida soldiers admitted into his ward, mostly from Finegan's brigade, and as early as mid-July he had begun to voice his deep concern for the welfare of his fellow Floridians. News of his concern quickly found its way to the trenches. W. A. wrote on July 27: "There has been as many as seventy five reported on the sick list in one morning I understand Dr. Palmer says if we are not sent back to the south we will all die."[6]

Three weeks later, on August 18, Dr. Palmer drafted a letter to the Confederate senators from Florida, James M. Baker and A. E. Maxwell. The letter was a long, heartfelt plea requesting that the new Florida brigade be returned home before the entire aggregate died of disease. From the moment the brigade arrived in Richmond in late May, he said, it had been reduced by two-thirds due to illness caused by an incompatible climate. He also stated that while serving in Florida, where the men were used to the sub-tropical climate, they offered a valuable service to the Confederacy.[7]

Howard's Grove Hospital served soldiers from the states of Alabama, Mississippi, Texas, Arkansas, and Florida. Dr. Palmer noted the Florida soldiers, although the lowest in aggregate numbers, suffered the highest mortality rate due to climatic influences.

I will give some facts to show that these Floridians suffer more from sickness here than either of the other states, because there are more new troops from Florida than from either of the other states. Texas and Arkansas have but few troops here, and they are all veterans, Mississippi and Alabama have many more than Florida, mostly veterans also. The numbers received into the hospital from each of those states are as follows: Alabama, 2,298; Mississippi, 925; Florida, 817; Texas, 295; Arkansas, 74. Alabama has about fifty regiments; Mississippi, about forty; Florida, six; Texas, three; and Arkansas, two; so that the proportion from Florida is far greater in proportion to the admissions. The admissions are about one-quarter, while the deaths are one-third, showing that Floridians die more rapidly than from these other states.

The composition of this brigade will also prove that it cannot be efficient in this climate under the fatigues which they are necessarily compelled to go through. First, it is composed of men over conscript age; second, men within conscript age who have been discharged from other commands in Virginia and Tennessee because they were unable to stand the hard service; third, boys under eighteen, a large number of whom have taken measles and will be unfit for service here for some months, and if they are furloughed they have to come back and go through the same acclimation as if they had never been here: all these facts go to prove that this brigade cannot do service in Virginia.

Dr. Palmer ended his petition with the assurance that Floridians could render a far greater service for the Confederacy if they were returned to Florida where they could defend their home state.

Acting on the concerns expressed in Dr. Palmer's letter, Florida Governor John Milton approved a legislative resolution the following December, demanding the return of Finegan's brigade to Florida. Again, the driving argument was rooted in the damaging influence of the harsh Virginia climate. Of course the governor had an ulterior motive. He feared another Federal assault comparable to the one which had threatened Olustee, and he wanted a full brigade to defend the state. Milton's greatest concern, however, was moving his men to a warmer winter climate to "recuperate their wasted health." The war department ignored the request, forcing the beleaguered brigade to endure in Virginia for the remainder of the war.[8]

Exactly how many men from the Ninth Florida Regiment died from disease while serving in Virginia trenches is unclear. Fourteen percent of the soldiers died while in Virginia, a total of ninety-one. However, some of these men died from effects of battle wounds and not illness—these numbers were small. The vast majority of hospital deaths were the unfortunate result of disease.[9]

They had arrived in Virginia at the worst time—late spring. The men found the weather extremely changeable, and in the end, deadly. In mid-June, W. A. complained that the weather was as cold as a winter day in Florida. "I get so cold at knight that I cant sleep." Hot, cold, wet, dry: this was an unusual summer as Virginia suffered from a drought stretching from mid-June to mid-July. Colonel Lang of the Eighth Florida Regiment complained, "there has not been rain enough to lay the dust here in more than a month and the crops are literally drying up while the dust is almost suffocating." The drought broke on July 18, when it rained the entire day. Then W. A. wrote, "It is so cold now at night that we have to get up and warm during the night."[10]

Sunday night, July 24, was particularly hard on the Florida troops. They were called from the comfort of their tents in reserve to occupy the open trenches of the front line. The night was cold and wet, and the wind blew so hard that W. A.'s hat repeatedly blew off his head. Then suddenly, the weather turned warm and clear. However, within two days rain threatened once again.[11]

August proved to be an extremely wet month. On August 22 Young wrote:

> For the last weak it has been raining eavry day we have had a bad time the ditches about half full of mud an water we would get wett eavry day an night it rained but very liddle yesterday an has not rained any to day I hope it will quit for atime for this is one of the worst places when it is wett that I eaver saw[12]

Not only did the Virginia climate inflict sickness and disease, but also it caused general discomfort for the soldier. " ... Rained all night I got wet an nearly eavery thing I had I neaver did spend a night as bad in my life as I did that night."[13] And there was no relief in sight.

Another force firing the Florida soldiers' dissatisfaction proved to be the disturbing reality that food rations were steadily diminishing as their days in the Old Dominion increased. The situation had not always been so grim. As late as June 16 Young informed his mother that although he had lost his belongings during the Battle of Cold Harbor, he could draw clothing whenever he wished. Flour bread, cornbread, bacon, coffee, sugar, peas, rice, onions, and tobacco were available. "We dont draw all of thease things at once but draw some at one time an some at anoather."[14]

The generous food supply was seriously reduced by early July, when rations were cut drastically. A deserter from the Florida Ninth Regiment explained to Federal officers that all his regiment received in rations per week was one-quarter pound bacon, three-quarters pound of cornmeal, and a little sugar and coffee. Suffering from the pinch W. A. wrote, "Our rations is getting verry short we dont get more than half as mutch as the men wants . . . I am fearful that we will have a hard time here in the way of eating."[15]

To combat their hunger many men from the regiment conducted foraging expeditions during the nights. Driven by gnawing hunger, these men killed anything in their paths, even "vegitables fare the same fate." Young joined one of these midnight parties. Although he never attended a hunting party, W. A. shared in the benefits. "I have a mess of fresh Beef for diner I didnt ask the man how he got it but could guess."[16]

Other rations grew short in supply also. On July 31, the day after the Battle of the Crater, Colonel Martin requested eighty-eight pairs of shoes and seventy-six pairs of pants. Colonel Martin also requisitioned 2,048 pounds of corn and 2,435 pounds of oats for "public animals and officers horses." Often the men of the Ninth were forced to purchase clothes from sutlers, hoping later to be reimbursed, but no mention is made of actual reimbursements. There were many requisitions for non-edible items also. Wood used to stoke the cooking fires as well as reinforcement for trenches and earthen fortresses was very scarce. On August 2, Company B requested one cord of wood to be used for cooking because the men had no wood to light fires to cook their meager rations.[17]

The cry of the hungry did not go unheard. On January 22, 1865, Finegan drafted a plea to his corps commander, General A. P. Hill, asking him to raise the daily bread allowance to one-quarter pound meal or eighteen ounces of flour per man. General Hill bluntly replied, "I believe that the ration is insufficient, yet nevertheless, other troops bear without complaint these evils they know we cannot help." Realizing that hunger was the main reason for Confederate desertions, he ended his response with a warning, "Also, I hold officers in charge of their regiments soley responsible for desertions."[18]

If A. P. Hill seemed cold and unfeeling in his response to General Finegan, another general who cared deeply for the well being of his men was drafting a letter to the secretary of war. Aware of the high desertion rate, and the causes of it, General Lee requested a sufficient food supply for his army. According to Lee, desertion would slow to a trickle if the troops were fed well and paid regularly. "There is suffering for want of food. The ration is too small for men who have to undergo so much exposure and labor as ours." Lee ended his appeal by suggesting that the "intelligence and experience on the part of the Commissary Department" think of a more efficient method of procuring supplies.[19]

Food was available through sutlers, townspeople, or truck farmers for exorbitant prices. In mid-August W. A. purchased six small peaches for $1.50. In July, cucumbers, barely two inches long, sold for $1.00 each, while common green apples sold for $2.00 to $3.00 per dozen, and, onion prices ranged from $.50 to $3.00 each. Young appropriately summed up the purchasing of foodstuffs by the hungry soldier; "eavery thing is so high that a soldier cannot buy any thing with his wages."[20]

Inflated prices were not limited to food products. W. A. lamented, "I cant get paper to read for less than fifty cents." In order for a Florida soldier to communicate with his family back home, he had to purchase paper and envelopes from the merchants in Petersburg. For a single pack of envelopes, a soldier was forced to pay $2.50 to $3.00, and paper was priced at $8.00 per quire. Soap was an impossible product to acquire. "We have to pay four to six dollars per for soap and then cant get it."[21]

During the early summer of 1864, as food rations grew scarce and merchants' prices inflated, the troops from Florida who had not succumbed to sickness began to consider desertion as an alternative to starvation.

Inconsistent pay disturbed soldiers also. Writing to General A. P. Hill in January 1865, General Finegan complained that his men had gone six months without pay. Hill responded that he could not help.[22]

Hardships were usually severe in Confederate ranks after Cold Harbor. From the moment of its arrival on May 25 to the end of the June campaigns near Ream's Station, the brigade was forced to march hundreds of miles within the Richmond area. On the 19 of June, W. A. wrote his wife of the increasing toll the exhausting marches exacted on his company.

I seat my self to let you know that I & Young is membered among the living: We are both broke down; we marched from near Malvern Hill on the other side of the James River about 25 or 30 miles to this place by five oclock yesterday Evening; and then we were a marching a long the lines to 12 oclock last night; I & Young made the trip; we had 61 men fit for duty yesterday morning out of the 61 thirty four got through last knight; Young and I got through[23]

With the workload increasing due to diminishing ranks, W. A. wrote six days later.

We are wore out we have been inline of battle a half a dozen times and marching day and night for the last 72 hours except last night we got to rest; I cant say how it [will] last I may finis this letter or may not I can say that no living man will last long and undergo the fatig we have to stand Young and me has been in every thing that our company has been in there is about fifteen or twenty of us that has held out the rest is sick or lazy and is stragling every day it makes the duty verry heavy on us[24]

In addition to the continuous forced marches, unrelieved skirmishing kept nerves exposed. "They fight aliddle some wheare on the lines eavry day but they call it skirmishing."[25]

Much of the time around Petersburg was spent constructing and fortifying the breastworks. Digging and building earthenworks was a draining job. Even when ordered to reserve, the men were required to stand picket.[26]

We are out a resting but in stead of resting we have to work and stand guard evry day & night witch brings it round to me a bout evry third day or night to work or stand guard our new company is suffering at a fearful rate[27]

W. A. wrote, "We get to sleep 2 1/2 hours at knight and then we don't get to sleep half enuff during the day."[28]

Frequent, yet unexpected, cannon bombardments of the enemy sent

W. A. from the luxury of his tent to the safety of a trench. "The shell has run me out of my tent in to the ditches they are bursting all around me now." Shelling was the cause of many wounds and deaths. "We sleep and cook out side of our trenches that is the cause [shelling] of those men being wounded."[29]

Even worse than enemy shellfire was the merciless aim of Union sharpshooters.

> I am tired of sharp shooting I understand that we got 40 men killed in two days by the sharp shooters; you may think something about forty men being killed here it is no more thought of than you would think about killing forty flies[30]

Anxiety for the safety of relatives and fellow Floridians added to the burden. On one such occasion, a detachment was feared captured, and when they finally returned to camp, a great joy rose throughout the brigade.[31]

Filth was probably the most demoralizing hardship the Florida soldiers were forced to endure. W. A. wrote, "I havent got but one suit of clothes an they are very black." Soap was a rare commodity. It could be purchased at exorbitant prices but rarely was received as a rationed item. Many soldiers resorted to washing their clothes without soap. Lice infested the hair and clothing of every soldier. "I think I can keep the lice down you may think that I am joking but I will assure you that they are plenty the way I kill them is to burn them I hold my shirt over the fire untill it gets verry hot."[32]

W. A. expressed his grief, "We have a hard time and no prospects of being better." Later he said, "Rebecca it is hard to have to leave all and suffer what I have to do."[33]

The younger soldiers suffered equally, but in different ways. The day after the Battle of Weldon Railroad Young confided to his mother:

> You dont no how anxious I am to get home I want this cruel war to stop so that we all can get home and live in peace I have been in three fights since I have been in Virginia an you cant imagine how bad I feel when I hafto go in to a fight I have neaver went in one yet but what I thought about you and all of my sisters and brothers you cant imagine what an awfull feeling it puts

on any one to go into a fight for one never knows what minute he will be shot down.[34]

Florida—it was their beloved Florida they yearned for. The vast majority failed to understand why they were removed from the palmettos and fresh breezes to the Confederate state most vulnerable to Union attack. Fear for the safety of loved ones and need to protect private property sent disgruntled soldiers heading south for home.

The Hunters were bound by the same Southern pride that enabled the war to last four long years. They didn't head for home. However, they made it known through many letters that they were equally homesick and genuinely concerned for the welfare of their kin back in Florida. They begin their letters with sentences like, "you dont know how I long to hear and see every thing that comes from home," and, "I received a letter from you yestarday . . . I was so glad to get it it is about all the pleasure I have but it only makes one want to get home worse."[35]

While it is true that the Floridians' fears of homes being destroyed and families being threatened by guerrillas are not much different from the fears of families near Pine Knob, Missouri or Helena, Arkansas, these other places had some recourse. Laws were enforced by occupying armies or local militias. The Florida families were virtually defenseless, and as the war wore on, the situation in Florida grew worse, not better, as it did further north.

Geography plays a significant role in shaping a soldier's view of strangeness and alienation. Soldiers from Indiana or Tennessee could feel a little " at home" in the midst of war in Virginia or North Carolina. But Florida's odd landscape, as odd as the moon's to Northerners, was home—and it was very different from that of Virginia to the men of the Ninth Florida. Was this different from the homesickness experienced by almost every Union and Confederate soldier in the Civil War? Probably not in tone, but certainly in degree.

Death was present in every letter W. A. Hunter wrote from the Virginia trenches. On one day, feeling low spirited and homesick, W. A. snipped a lock of hair from Young's head and his own and sent it to Rebecca as a lasting remembrance.[36]

Still, the world of the living was very much on his mind. By letter he instructed Rebecca about which fields to plow, which crops to plant, and where to sell the harvest. In early July, W. A. was devastated when he heard from recent arrivals that the entire corn crop in northern Florida had been destroyed by rain.

The inflated national currency—bad Confederate money—proved to be a constant annoyance for W. A. He instructed Rebecca to hide the gold and trade in Confederate money. W. A. said, "Floridan currency is good only to pay tax and buy land it aint worth a fig out side of the state." Another financial problem arose when W. A. tried to collect his debts. Asa A. Stewart, the former Captain of Company E, owed W. A. for a slab of bacon. "If Captain Stewart wont pay in Florida money as mutch as you think proper take it in the new Ishue Confederate not less than $3." It is not known whether Captain Stewart ever paid his debt.[37]

The family's recalcitrant slave, Dane, threatened Rebecca and the children. W. A. instructed his wife:

As for Dane if he cant behave him self you had better get the advice of some of the men in the settlement if he dont do better you had better have him sold or he will be hung and if he is to go in the house to any one of course he would be hung or ought to be hung I would let him know that I intended to put the law in force against him it may give him a scare tell Arthur to watch him and I want Chastun to give a severe whiping[38]

Two days later he again wrote: "Try to scare Dane and if he wont behave him self you must kill him or sell him be sure you keep the children safe tell Melissa & Sue to shoot him." The problem with Dane persisted as evidenced in the following excerpt from W. A. dated August 4, 1864:

You said that Dane wouldn't come home of mornings; If he wont do get JC Young or some one to swap or sell him; If you was to let him know that you would sell him he might do better I would tell the children that I would sell him if he didn't do better and see what effect it would take on him; The first thing to have Chastun or some man to whip him severely if he don't do better.[39]

A possible enemy advance on Lake City, identical to that during the Olustee campaign of February 1864, was always present in the minds of the Floridians. Olustee had been a Florida victory, but now Florida's fighting men were no longer within the state's boundaries to repeat their victory. Two days after the Battle of Cold Harbor, W. A. heard that a Federal expedition had left Jacksonville intent on capturing Lake City. Quickly, rumors spread throughout the trenches that Lake City had been burned, and that the Yankees had overrun the area. However, he was to learn later, that the small Federal force was easily pushed back to Union-occupied Jacksonville.[40]

In August Federal troops in Jacksonville targeted Gainesville as their objective on yet another expedition to capture the heart of Florida. Again, rumors raged within the ranks. W. A. instructed Rebecca:

> I hear the Yankees was invading Fla; I am fearful we will lose all I want you to do what you think is best for you and the children if your neighbors leave I want you to try and get off if you can; and if they dont leave you can do as well as they can do; I cant say what would be the best for you to do; can you do anything with the cotton; see Miot and J.C. Young [Rebecca's brother] and see if they can store it a way by sending it up the railroad or whether they can sell it.. Take care of your hard money be sure you keep it out of the hands of any person; Yankees or any person else; as for the negroes if you think it best to run them off do as you think best.[41]

By late 1864 the Florida swamp holdouts, Yankee sympathizers, and Confederate deserters, with support from the Union blockade, were leading ever-more-frequent raiding parties on the civilian population of the state. The Florida Brigade, struggling daily with fears that their families and fortunes were suffering at the hands of these perfidious renegades, had reached the breaking point. Many soldiers, unable to withstand the torment, secretly stole away, determined to return to their homes in Florida and deal with whatever was threatening there.[42]

Lieutenant Sam Worthington of Company A resigned his commission and returned to Florida. "I have a helpless family consisting of twelve," he said, " all females except one 2 year old boy . . . robbed of all support." Within the state of Florida, leaders feared for the safety of the civilian population also. When Finegan's force was ordered to Virginia, Florida Governor John Milton's aide-de-camp penned a letter of protest to the War Department in Richmond:

All men count . . . Torries threaten us from the South, the Yankee Coasters from the Gulf on the west, the Yankees and Negroes from Fort Butler on the east and nothing comes from above but sundry orders contradictory and perplexing. We are without troops to defend us. Those of us at home are constantly doing military duty. Our county resembles a camp where orders against circulating false rumors are not enforced, nor is the enemy inactive. Under these circumstances we are trying to make a crop and save ourselves from the tender mercies of our fanatic neighbors who would not sell us corn for Confederate money.[43]

Why the Confederacy allowed such free Union troop movements in a Confederate state remained a painful mystery to all Floridians. Perhaps the answer lay in an observation written by a non-Floridian, Major E. C. Holcombe. "I have reached Florida . . . a very poor and uninteresting country. There is nothing of interest going on in this army that I know of, everything dull and quiet."[44] Florida was too far from the theater of war, and, many Confederate leaders thought, not worth saving.

But the deepest reason for the poor troop morale had to be that by the end of the summer of 1864 the men knew that all they were doing for the cause would be in vain. General fear of the enemy was prevalent and unreliable rumors in the camps spread quickly throughout the brigade and heightened fears for safety. Lee's army weakened daily with little hope of replenishment, whereas Grant's army was able to refill its ranks. This obvious advantage of manpower disturbed the men. W. A. painted the picture:

Yesterday the Yankee wagons could be seen by hundreds moving our officers couldn't make out what it meant to find out whether they were gone or not they opened all our batterys on them and the boys raised a yell as if we were charging them they soon showed themselves behind there works they appear to be as numerous as the ants is in Florida at one of there hills.[45]

Rumors helped promote disloyalty among the ranks also. In July, General Jubal Early conducted an expedition on Washington. Rumors rushed through the camps like a mighty gust of wind. Many men believed they would be forced to march to Maryland. "I am as far north as I want to go," W. A. commented. Colonel David Lang of the Eighth Florida Regiment believed Early's raid on Maryland was a ruse to draw Grant's infantry away from Petersburg, or an expedition to collect cattle, horses, and supplies along the way. "This being the object, his campaign has been a success; otherwise it has failed!" Colonel Lang's summation of Early's sortie epitomized the anxious mood of the entire Florida Brigade.[46]

There was very low or no pay to do all these impossible jobs. Without money, the common Florida soldier could not supplement his meager weekly ration when the monthly pay was colonel, $175.00; lieutenant colonel, $170.00; major, $150.00; captain, $100.00; 1st lieutenant, $90.00; 2nd lieutenant, $80.00; sergeant, $14.00; and finally private, $11.00. Lack of cash, high prices, and poor treatment caused the Florida troops to loathe their situation. Complaining of exorbitant prices to his sister, Melissa, Young wrote:

> Eavery thing is so high that a soldier cannot buy anything with his wages I never wanted to get home so bad in my life a soldier is not treated as good heare as a dog is at home but I hope we will soon get home a gain I think if I get out of this war that I will not get in another one soon.

W. A. agreed with his son. He felt strongly that equality was lacking in the Confederate army. W. A. stated, "the ritch can an does get all the spoils."[47]

There was, of course, punishment for the soldier if he offended. On one particular evening a detachment of soldiers was forced out of the trenches. Writing to Rebecca W. A. stated, "we have to fight untill we drive the Yankees away; or we get whip." From W. A.'s point of view Colonel John M. Martin of the Ninth Regiment treated his men harshly. "I cant tell you how mean our Col. Treats us; but there will be a change sometime."[48]

By July frayed nerves began to shred among the Florida Brigade. W. A.'s state of mind sank into apathy, as did the morale of many of his compatriots. Hatred for the war, Virginia, and their rich officers intensified. One day, after Union shells forced the men from their tents and into the trenches, W. A. confided to Rebecca, "I am not satisfied nor never will be as long as I have to stay in Virginia I dont like it and the service I hate and shall hate untill my death; let it be soon or late."[49]

Many men believed all problems would be solved immediately if only the Florida troops were sent home. In late July Young wrote:

> If they would send Finegans Brigade back we would keep the Yanks and deserters out of the state during the war . . . their is adeale of dissatisfaction in the Brigade several have went to the Yanks . . . a great many of them are sick and several has died.[50]

Exactly one month later Young expressed an even deeper concern for his home state.

> I hear that East Florida is expected to be evacuated an given up to the Yanks I hope it is not so Florida has as much right for protection as any oather state an I think she ought to have it she has done as much for the Confederacy according to her population as any oather state an their fore she ought to have protection.[51]

There was hope within Finegan's brigade that their return to Florida would happen before winter set in. W. A. wrote in August:

> Our Brigade is trying to be sent back; and if they dont send us there will be one half of them that desert and try to get back to Florida we are in hopes of being sent back in the course of four weeks; I do hope and pray to the Lord that they will send us back forthwith.

Even the responsible W. A. had a boiling point. He wrote, "if there aint some change in affairs and treatment here to the soldier I am fearful the desertion will be commin."[52]

Following John M. Martin's promotion to colonel, and Major Pickens Bird's death at Cold Harbor, the Ninth Regiment had two high-ranking vacancies: lieutenant colonel and major. These vacancies remained open until the end of the war. On September 6, 1864, Colonel Martin wrote General Samuel Cooper requesting that Captains Tucker and Hope fill the regimental vacancies: Tucker, lieutenant colonel and Hope, major. The promotions failed to materialize mainly because General Finegan hoped to fill the positions with outsiders. This prompted a verbal duel between Finegan and Martin. Colonel Martin felt promoting outsiders was not justified—Tucker and Hope had proven their gallantry within the unit.[53]

Tedious inspections were routine. Because of heavy work details and battle anxiety, the men were weary, and the last thing they cared to prepare for was an inspection. Sometimes an inspection for the Florida men meant firing their guns, then cleaning them, and other times it included General Lee or General Beauregard conducting a scrutinizing inspection of their lines. On one such occasion the generals concluded that the Florida front was too frail to withstand a Federal assault and ordered the lines strengthened immediately.[54]

The reports left behind an invaluable legacy of specific material from the trenches at this time. These reports confirm that sanitary conditions were bad. The men suffered from "itch, for want of soap," and insufficient clothing. The field infirmary was supplied "indifferently," and accommodations for the sick were also "indifferent." During the winter months scurvy was prevalent, and many men suffered from pneumonia, primarily due to exposure. If a Florida soldier had money to buy food or new clothes, he had to journey far afield. The inspection reports show there were no sutlers in Finegan's command.

Much-needed spiritual leadership and guidance was also lacking in the brigade. It was not until December 1864 that the Ninth Regiment had a spiritual leader, the Reverend James Little. The inspection reports reveal another interesting fact: twice a month the common soldiers were ordered to read the articles of war, and upon occasion they were forced to recite army regulations and tactics. Such a demand upon this highly illiterate group must have been infuriating.[55]

Debilitating disease and sickness, the tedium of brigade inspections, the lack of payment, and the dearth of rations all contributed to one final act for eighteen percent of the men from the Ninth Florida Regiment, the act of desertion. Eighteen percent is also the statistic for all regiments comprising Finegan's brigade. The companies comprising the Ninth Florida had organized as militiamen in Florida, and they often retained the militiaman mentality. These men left the army when it was inconvenient to stay, such as during an enemy attack, or when they were forced to return from a furlough, or more likely, to go home to harvest a crop. These in-state desertions, 176 of them, were not pleasing to the army, as proven by the action taken in the case of Isaac J. Wiley.[56] Wiley was a brevet 2nd lieutenant from Company H, where he commanded a detachment of troops guarding Black Creek. On March 16, 1864 he deserted. Later he was found, arrested, and on April 15, 1864, was hanged for his crime.

As the group had reflected on leaving their homeland for Virginia, another bunch deserted by catching the transport train. According to Isham Cooper, a corporal in Company D, Tenth Florida Regiment, when the train stopped in Lake City, he and sixty to seventy others jumped off and deserted to the Union forces in Jacksonville.[57]

The exact number of men belonging to the Ninth Florida who deserted while serving in Virginia may never be known. However, a figure close to the truth is 121 men with approximately 125 others reported absent without leave. Though desertion is never to be countenanced in any efficient war effort, it is interesting to see that it was not necessarily a natural concomitant of the character of the Florida men. Desertion was blasphemous to them during the first month of their stay in Virginia. They were not hungry then because rations were plentiful, sickness had not yet gripped their ranks, and constant marches kept scenery fresh and tempers soothed. It was not until the month of July that desertion became more common. [58]

The *Official Records of the War of Rebellion* cites the Ninth, Tenth, and Eleventh Florida Regiments infrequently. Yet when the Florida regiments are mentioned, it records Union correspondence concerning Rebel deserters fleeing to their lines. On July 14, three "stupid and unintelegent" soldiers from the Ninth deserted to the enemy. As desertions increased, deserters were quick to inform Federal troops of Rebel intelligence.[59]

In spite of the threat of hanging, when cold weather set in, the number of desertions increased. During the period between November 20 and December 1, twenty-seven Floridians deserted Confederate ranks. By the end of 1864, cold weather, lack of proper clothing, exposure, hunger, and the failure to be paid stoked their desire to desert in greater numbers.[60]

Bound less closely to the Confederate cause by virtue of their frontier background and desperation, these deserters fled to Federal lines nightly. They grew to be annoyances as they continually awakened Union officers at all hours of the night pleading for sanctuary. The Sixty-third Pennsylvania harbored so many deserters from Finegan's brigade that a ranking officer sent General Finegan the following note: "Come over and take command of your Brigade, most of which is apparently on our side of the entrenchments; or if not convenient to come personally, to have your details report promptly before 9 o'clock PM." Finegan quickly responded by shelling the Sixty-third's lines for ten hours straight. Desertion was not accepted lightheartedly, however. The ranking officers of Finegan's brigade were deeply concerned about the mounting wave of deserters. When the opportunity presented itself, punitive measures were taken to instill fear in all the men. Young witnessed one such occasion. He recorded, in a letter to Melissa, a lasting impression of an execution as seen through the eyes of a confused eighteen-year-old.[61]

> Our Brigade was caled on to witness aseeane [a scene] today that I never will forget their was two men from Company C, 11th Florida Regiment shot to death for desertion they were tied with their backs to a stake their coffins placed a few feet in the rear of them their graves were dug about ten spaces in the reaer when all was ready twenty-four men were drawn up in a line and orders were given to fire the poor fellows were shot up it made me feal bad but I could not help them now.[62]

By the end of the war 121 soldiers from the Ninth Regiment had deserted, totaling eighteen percent of its strength. Also, 125 men were reported absent without leave, nineteen percent of the total force. Of the 656 men belonging to the Ninth Regiment and serving in Virginia, 246 left the ranks illegally. This constituted a combined thirty-eight percent desertion rate from the entire Florida Brigade.[63]

General William Mahone was forced to leave the Florida Brigade behind in the trenches while he led his division into action during the Battle of the Crater. "Honor" and "duty" seemed empty words in the summer of 1864. All the Florida men wanted was home.

7.

DON'T GRIEVE FOR ME

During July 1864, the Ninth Regiment regularly shifted its position between the front and reserve lines near Petersburg. On the blustery night of July 20, the regiment was ordered to the front trenches just east of Jerusalem Plank Road and approximately one-half mile south of Elliott's Salient. There it remained for the balance of the month.[1]

In many places east of Petersburg the Confederate trenches ran in proximity to the Northerner's lines. No point exemplified this more than the Confederate strongpoint located on Elliott's Salient, near Blanford Church and Cemetery Hill. Here picket lines were less than four hundred feet apart. Perched atop the salient, Peagram's South Carolina Artillery, a group of seasoned veterans, commanded a battery of four guns. Lining the entrenchment on both sides of Peagram were the Twenty-second and the Eighteenth South Carolina Regiments.[2]

Down the long slope, across from Elliott's Salient, the Union embankment lay carved on the crest of a ravine. At the bottom of the ravine lay the tracks of a railroad line, with General Ambrose Burnside and his Ninth Corps commanding these lines. General Burnside, wishing to clear his name of the stain of his Fredericksburg campaign, was desperate to break the stalemate facing him. In December 1862 he had ordered his troops to storm an impenetrable stone wall held by the tenacious Lee. Wave after wave of his men went to slaughter. In July of 1864 he was looking for one final opportunity to vindicate himself and to become a hero. He needed an idea—an unusual plan to break the Rebel lines.

The Forty-eighth Pennsylvania was stationed directly across from the salient. The Forty-eighth consisted primarily of coal miners commanded by Lieutenant Colonel Henry Pleasants, a coal-mining engineer by profession. One day, while walking through the ranks and pondering a solution to this war of attrition, Pleasants overheard one of his men say, "We could blow that . . . fort out of existence if we could run a mine shaft under it." That simple statement sparked a plan in Pleasant's mind. He quickly devised a scheme to dig a gallery some five hundred feet to a point under Elliott's Salient.[3] Under Confederate lines, a huge explosive charge would be set to blow an enormous opening in the lines. Northern troops, taking advantage of the element of stunned surprise, were to pour around the crater and take Petersburg, thus ending the war.

After truly ingenious digging, shafting, and deceiving of the Confederates, at the end of July, the plan was complete for Burnside to implement with battlefield action. All he needed to do was order the engineer corps to remove the obstructions between the lines after darkness fell, so his troops could pass freely through the barricades between the lines when the explosion occurred.

A few days earlier General Grant had sent a body of troops north to pester Richmond in a ruse, forcing Lee to split his army in defense of the Confederate capitol city. Grant's plan worked. On the morning of July 30, only 18,000 Confederate soldiers were left to guard Petersburg.[4]

The stage was set for a great Union victory and a quick end to the long war. A half mile away the Hunters and the Ninth Florida Regiment were called into battle array at 3:30 AM. There they stood and watched. What they saw was dreadful.[5]

In the confusion, mayhem and military mismanagement that followed at the explosion and Battle of the Crater, thousands of Northern and Southern soldiers were killed, dismembered, or otherwise horribly injured, and the North's plan lay in ruins.

For the North the results were devastating. One month of hard labor by Pleasants and his men was foolishly wasted. Instead of rushing on to Petersburg as planned, the assaulting forces had stopped and filled the crater, losing the battle. The Black division of General Ferrarro had drilled for a month prior to the charge. If plans had not been altered, it is probable the Black forces would have reached Petersburg. As a result of this debacle Major General Ambrose E. Burnside was relieved of command. General Grant wrote:

> The assaulting column, formed of the Ninth Corps, immediately took possession of the Crater made by the explosion, and the line for some distance to the right and left of it, and a de-

tached line in front of it, but for some cause failed to advance promptly to the ridge beyond. Had they done this, I have every reason to believe that Petersburg would have fallen . . . Thus terminated in disaster what promised to be the most successful assault of the campaign.[6]

How did the Floridians, who were left behind, view the battle? For hours the Ninth Regiment witnessed the slaughter of the Crater. The following day W. A. recorded what he saw:

I hasten to write you a few lines to let you know that my self and Young is a mong the living. Yankes charged our lines yesterday on the left of our brigade and we fought them for about five hours. I will let you know the particulars of it They dug under our lines and at day light they made the attack with five lines of battle. Our General had found out that the attack was to be made and had that part of the lines reenforced as it was the nearest to the Yanks we were put in battle areay at 3 in the morning. At day light they put a slow match and made the charge the explosion took place and blew up about thirty yards of our line with the men that was our front we had three lines there killing and burying up our poor men unthought of our lines gave way to take care of them selves. The Yanks had run up so close that they lost nearly as many men as we did by the explosion they took possession of that part of our lines and open up on us the most terrifying canonading at most ever was heard the shells flew as thick as hail from mortars and all the different kinds of canon they threw shrapnell & canister & grape shot & solid shot for a bout five hours as long as the engagement lasted up to that time they held our blew up line we had drove them back to their lines at all other points it remained so with a pretty severe canonade to about two oclock in the evening then our troops (Willcocks & Mahones [Weisinger's] & Wrights Brigades) made a charge on the Yanks in our captured lines. They retaken the lines and taken about one to two thousand prisoners & our Brigade was not charged by the Yanks so we were not in the fight except the shells they flew all around all the way. I can give you my idea of it is in the time of a thunderstorm in Florida were there is a greadeal of dead pine timber that comes to the nearest to it of anything that I every heard there was none of our company hurt I cant tell you what our loss is verry heavy. Stanhope Harris is just in from the field he says the dead is lying every where and we are busy a digging them out of the dirt wrights Brigade suffered the worst they are Georgia troops they had to come in under the Canonading; I cant tell you our loss is you will see it in the papers before you get this and as soon as I learn more about it I will let you know the attack was to have been a general one but the yanks failed to make it; our battle lines is about twenty miles long or may be thirty as they extend on the other side of the James River; among the yanks there is a good number of negroes we have the yankee negroes a burrying and diging the dead out of the ground; I think the yanks got worsted in the fight; I think they will get worsted evry time they try to charge us. I cant tell how soon they will try our whole line the only way they can take our lines is to beat them down with the canon and when they undertake that they will fail for we have some verry heavy pieces of canon;…I must bring my letter to a close we are on some duty evry knight young is on picket at this time he went on last knight I don't know when I will have to go;…I must get me something to eate; fare well if I meet you no more in this life I hope to meet you in the land where there will be no more parting or sorrow or pain; . . . [7]

The following morning General Finegan ordered his men into battle array very early in anticipation of another Union assault. Later, when it was obvious there would be no fight, W. A. continued his letter from the previous day:

Young and my self is well this morning as comin; all is quiet on our lines this morning we are in line of battle and has been since three this morning we form line everry morning at three oclock and remain in line to sunrise; all the news that I can gather from the explosion; is the 22 South Carolina was one of the Reg. That was blown up; we dident loss verry many by the explosion. [8]

After losing the Battle of the Crater, Grant no longer attempted a direct assault on Petersburg. His focus shifted to severing the supply

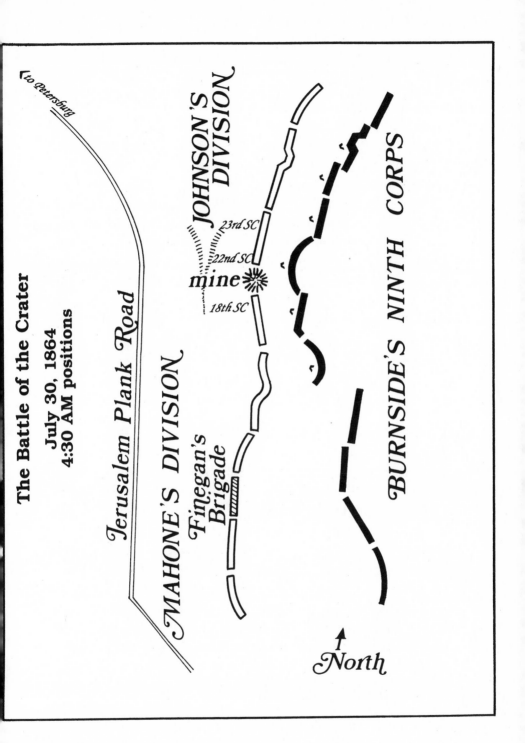

The Battle of the Crater

July 30, 1864
4:30 AM positions

to Petersburg

Jerusalem Plank Road

MAHONE'S DIVISION

Finegan's Brigade

JOHNSON'S DIVISION

23rd SC

22nd SC

mine

18th SC

BURNSIDE'S NINTH CORPS

North

lines into the vital city. In the Florida trenches, what feeling there was of battle victory quickly dissolved as the hot and hungry days of August wore on. It was dangerous even in the defenses. When the fetid atmosphere of the trenches grew too stifling, the soldiers emerged from the entrenchments to cook and sleep and were rudely met with deadly fire from the barrels of Federal sharpshooters.[9]

With only occasional sniper fire and artillery blasts, the first half of August passed mostly in marked silence along both lines. The Confederates continued to hold the ground they had occupied since the day of July 30. Each morning the Ninth Regiment mustered into a line of battle at three in the morning and remained there until sunrise. By August 11, Finegan's brigade extended its line across the Jerusalem Plank Road. By mid-August many Confederate brigades had pulled out of the trenches. Members of Finegan's brigade complained that the pullout placed their safety in jeopardy; by August 15 there remained but a single brigade protecting their right flank.[10]

On August 3, W. A. wrote Rebecca after receiving a welcome letter from her. Concerning his eating habits he described his unusual diet:

> I am as well as I get I have been eating some peaches (green ones cooked) and some corn verry young and some watermelons (green ones) and a little rice and fresh beef all cooked together; you may know I am feeling better or I couldn't eat sutch stuff; Young is not well today but able to do duty

For quite some time W. A. had asked Rebecca to send needles and thread to him.

> . . .got a pair of suspenders & some thread and one needle & some thread in the letter they came in a verry good time as I needed them; I drawn a pair of pants the other day they havent got as many buttons on them as I wanted now I will sew the buttons on them. I can pick up plenty of buttons here Send me the socks and a pair of gloves as soon as you can I have a pair of fine Yankee socks They are too thin for this country.

Knowing that he and Young would need new boots for the winter months, W. A. instructed Rebecca to have shoes made.

Rebecca have you got Mr. Guinn to make any more shoes or have you said any thing to him about it If you get him have a pair made for myself and Young have them made some little longer than the last ones was made and made out of the best leather and two rows of pibs put in and high quarters stifened behind and raised high in the instep and keep them untill we want them

Following the Battle of the Crater rumors of more Union mines spread through Confederate camps.

I have no news all is quiet since the fight on Saturday; Each party is strenghening there works and watching each other; it is said the Yankees is digging under they found at different places; our men are at the same I expect some one will be blown up before verry long; I under stand we had got nearly under the Yankees the other day The Yanks found it out; Our men were out and the Yankees dug a hole in to the mine This is camp news I cant vouch for it; I know we are trying to under mine them; and I believe they are at the same work in different places[11]

The next day W. A. emphasized the importance of preventing Grant from extending Union lines.

The firing was very heavy last knight this morning all appears to be quiet; I think the Yankees is trying to extend their line of breast works to the Rail Road between Petersburg & Weldon if they try that we will have some warm work for it is verry essential to us to hold the Road for a good portion of our supplies come on that Road; I would be glad they would leave here for I am tyard of lying here in the ditches we have pretty hard times but we don't have to make them long marches

Foodstuffs were growing scarce and again W. A. expressed his concern:

Our rations is verry short but as good or better than they were at Lake City except in bread we don't get enuff of bread here;

They give us corn and flour bread corn peas and rice sugar and coffee Bacon & Pickled pork & Beef salt & soap & tobacco; but not enuff of any except tobacco we get plenty of that;

To make matters worse the weather in August started out quite hot:

We are having some verry warm wether we are in an old field where there is no shade whitch makes it verry warm there is some rain about As soon as we get a good rain it will be as cold as winter is in Florida

W. A. had "hope" that sustained him through the worst of times, yet as he closed his letter dated August 4, there was a definite hint of pessimism when he wrote, "Kiss my babes for me Tell them where the poor old father is."[12]

Constantly fighting health problems, W. A. reported to Rebecca on the fifth that he and Young were suffering:

Young is not well he reported on the sick list this morning; it is his bowels he don't look well; I am all right except I eate too mutch green corn and that puts me all rong[13]

In late July and early August a Federal force in Jacksonville advanced westward. This caused high levels of anxiety among the Florida troops in Virginia because they were concerned for the welfare of their families back home. Fortunately the daring Captain J.J. Dickison turned the Federal force back to Jacksonville after meeting the enemy near Gainesville. News of this Union expedition reached the trenches. W. A. wrote with grave concern on August 14:

... why don't you write and let me know what you are doing and how near the yankees is to you and what you propose to do do you expect to stay or do you expect to leave if you can; I am anxious to hear from you[14]

Again concerned with the close proximity of the Yankees to his family, the next day W. A. drafted one more letter to the now very pregnant Rebecca:

Camp Near Petersburg Va Aug 15 1864

Dear Wife

I seat my self on my knapsack to write a few lines to you; I have just received yours of the 4 & 5 I was glad to hear from you again I hadent heard from you since Mr D Bryant come; I was more anxious to hear as I hear the Yankees was invading Fla; I am fearful we will loss all I want you to do what you think is best for you and the children if your neighbors leav I want you to try and get off if you can; and if they don't leave you can do as well as they can do; I cant say what would be the best for you to do; Can you do any thing with the cotton; see Miot and J C Young and see whether they can store it a way by sending it up the Rail Road or whether they can sell it; it might be that you could store it up a bout Madison. See them and hear what they think a bout it; take care of your hard money be sure you keep it out of the hands of any person; yankees or any person else; as for the negroes if you think it best to run them off do as you think best; what is Dr Parcks and Miot & Hagin and all of your neighbors a going to do; you must be your own judge. Our Brigade is trying to be sent back; and if they don't send us there will be one half of them that will desert and try to get back to Florida; we loss some men everry night by desertion we are in hopes of being sent back in the course of four weeks; I do hope and pray to the Lord that they will send us back forthwith; we have some verry warm whether & last night we had a heavy rain to day we are out of the trenches untill seven o clock this evening; Our troops is leaving hear and going toward Richmond I dont know where they go to; we may have to follow as there is but one Brigade on our right now; some think the Yankees is a leaving. I cant say more than I saw plenty of them this morning at there breast works; Young is gone out in the country to get some thing to eate to day; I paid one dollar and a half for six small peaches to day they were the first that have eate; my health is bad every thing I eate disagrees with me; Young is better looks poor and yellow; I am going send this by Mr Scott that same boy that carried the mail from Lake City to Newnansville last year; kiss my babes and tell all the rest howdy for me; give my love to Rosannah & W & A & W Buford is well and all the rest from your settlement give my respects to all of my old friends; Rebecca it is hard to have to leave all and suffer what I have to do; but I hope the Lord will provide for you and me; don't grieve I have a hope that keeps me up I hope we will meet again;[15]

Your Husband
W A Hunter

On the sixteenth of August Rebecca went into labor. Before the end of the day she gave birth to a beautiful baby girl, born while the child's "Poor old father" suffered in the filth of the Petersburg trenches. The baby was christened Willie Annie Hunter, bringing pleasure to Rebecca and the oldest daughters, Melissa and Susannah.

Work details continued to drain the beleaguered Ninth Regiment. Continuous picket duty combined with arduous, eternal details prompted W. A. to paint a vivid picture:

I must close to go to picket all though today is the sabbath . . . tell Mrs. Bryant that her brother Sam is all right for he is standing on the breast work calling for his detail to work I belong to it.[16]

Pressing onward with his new strategy, General Grant now attempted to disrupt the Confederate supply line via the Weldon Railroad route. A Union force was amassed near Globe Tavern along the Weldon line. On the morning of August 21, Finegan's brigade marched down the Weldon line to meet the enemy at Globe Tavern. In the sweltering heat of the afternoon, they charged the enemy. The initial charge was quickly repelled with heavy Southern casualties. An entire brigade was caught inside an angle of the Union line and ripped to shreds, with 681 soldiers going into the battle and only 274 emerging.[17]

General Mahone was not quickly discouraged, however, and promptly ordered a second assault. In this charge, the Ninth Regiment stormed across a trampled cornfield. The grape shot, canister, and minié balls flew "thick as hail," and cornstalks exploded into dust when struck. The Ninth Regiment was locked into the center of the "hottest fight" it had ever been in. It was during this fiery charge that W. A. was struck down by a minié ball. The ball passed through the calf of his right leg and lodged in the bone of the left leg. Young was close to his father. He dropped his musket and carried W. A. to the rear where the litter bearers removed him from the battlefield.[18]

This second assault collapsed miserably about the time W. A. was wounded, and Mahone gave the order to fall back. A section of the Weldon line near Globe Tavern had passed into Union hands at the cost of many Southern lives.

Other casualties of the Battle of Weldon Railroad included two important Floridians. The colorful Captain John Wiley Pearson of Company B was severely wounded. On September 1, 1864, he resigned his commission and left for Florida. In Augusta, Georgia, he succumbed to his wounds. Also one of the sons of General Finegan, a lieutenant, was slightly wounded in the battle and sent to the hospital in Richmond.[19]

W. A. was a well-liked, respected man whose strength of character had impressed the younger soldiers. One wrote a letter to Mrs. Hunter:

I take my pen to write you a few lines this evening with much reluctance I write you at present our regiment was called into a fight the twenty first of this month I must say to you Mr Hunter got wounded in that fight Got wounded in the leg in the back part of the leg below the knee and the other in the front that one the front of the leg the bone is severed some but not broken . . . He went in the fight close by me on the first of the fight we were repulse the first time then the order was to fall back then made a second charge we went close together the last time I seen him and Young he was down on his knees shot I went in front of him some fifty yards of the battery and went to shoot shot some three times Look back and seen that our men all had left then I left that place . . . went out the same way and seen some of the boys Young had got his father . . . He is at the brigade hospital will be sent to Richmond . . . I think that Mister Hunter will be able to go home in a few weeks if his wounds is not bad so I understand he will be able to get a furlough[20]

After assisting his father off the battlefield, Young returned to his company. Despair crept deeper into the hearts and minds of many of Finegan's men. They had failed to dislodge the Yankees from the major supply line, and now the vital railroad would be torn up. Thoughts of fighting a losing battle filled their minds. For Young life in camp would change. He no longer had his father's wisdom, love, and protection to fall back upon. Was there anything more that could be taken away?

8.

THE LAND WHERE PAIN IS NOT KNOWN

The day after the Battle of Weldon Railroad, August 22, following his stint on picket duty, Young drafted a letter to his mother:

I am sorry to inform you that Pa was wounded yestarday in boath legs below the neas the ball went through the calf of the right leg and struck the bone of the left leg but did not break it I don't think he is any way dangerously wounded we ware charging the yankes breast works when he was wounded an about the time he was wounded we ware ordered to fall back I went to Pa and brought him out to the River we made two charges and had to fall back boath times we lost a great many men boath times the breast works we ware charging are about four miles from this place the yankees went down on the Weldon R. Road four or five days ago an fortified an yestarday Anderson Division went down an tried to charge them out but we ware repulsed it was the hottest fight I have been in to yet the yankees ware well fortified an we had to charge through an open corn field the shell grape canister an minie balls come as thick as haill the last charge we made (the one Pas was wounded in) it looked to me like eavry stalk of corn in the field was struck I think we came out lucky to not loose no more men than we did our Co. went in the fight with a bout thirty men and lost four men wounded an one killed Stanhope Harress was out at the Hospittal last night and came in this morning he told me that Pas was adoing as well as cold be expected they sent him to the field Hospittal this morning and from theire I expect he will be sent on to day to Richmond I hope he will be sent to Richmond for the wounded are treded better their than they are heare at Petersberg if his wound does well I think he will get home in two or three weeks on furlough I hope he may get a furlough and get home he received the letter that you sent the money in an the money that was the last one he got from you[1]

On August 24 Young wrote to his sister, Melissa, further describing the horrible scene of battle on the twenty-first:

> The Yankees had flanked us and taken possession of the Rail road an we went down to try to drive them away from the road but when we went we found them strongly fortified and a great many more men than we had but we ware ordered to charge their works but alass it was all in vain we made two charges an were drive back both times with the loss of a great many men we had to charge through an open cornfield in the last charge we made was the one Pa was wounded in about the time he was wounded we ware ordered to fall back but as good luck would have it I was near him an went to him and brought him out under a hevy fire if I had not brought him out he would fell into the hands of the enemy the Yanks whipped us nicely but we will give it to them yet I am afraid there will be some hard fighting around Petersburg.[2]

After Young removed his father from the battlefield, W. A. was hoisted onto a litter and carried to one of the ambulances waiting in the rear. From there he was transported over bumpy roads to the field hospital five miles to the north. This was the dreaded brigade hospital of which W. A. had written so vehemently the previous month, where there was no shade and no one to get the pitiful wounded a drink of water. He remained at the field hospital for two days, lying on the open ground and suffering. The bullet was removed from his leg, but the leg through which the minié ball had passed was beginning to fester. He waited quietly, patiently for his turn to be transported to the Richmond hospital. There was no hatred now toward officers, doctors, or the deplorable conditions of the primitive and filthy brigade hospital.

Finally, on the August 23 W. A. was transported to Richmond and admitted into the Florida Ward, Ward K of the First Division of Howard's Grove Hospital. This was the ward managed by the compassionate Dr. Thomas M. Palmer of Monticello, who the previous month had drafted a letter to the Florida senators pleading for the return home of the Florida troops.[3]

Waiting to receive W. A. was Dr. T. C. Griffin, a friend of the

Hunter family, the same Dr. Griffin W. A. believed had escaped to Richmond to get "out of the way of bullets." Doctor Griffin examined W. A.'s wounds and found the infection had spread ominously. In a letter to Young, Griffin stated:

> When he reached here last eavning there were signs of gangrene about his wounds. This morning his leg was black to his knee and he showed evident signs of spreading. Nothing could be done for him as he was prostrated when he reached here.[4]

W. A., still clinging to the hope of life beyond earth, remained in good spirits. As an encouragement to Dr. Griffin, W. A. was very happy, "declaring that he would soon be released from all his trouble."[5]

The following morning, August 24, 1864, at approximately 8:00, W. A. succumbed to his mortal infection and quietly passed away. At his bedside was a dear family friend, Jacob C. Miller. At the very second of W. A.'s death, Miller was drafting a letter to Rebecca to inform her of her husband's grave condition:

> Mrs. Rebecca Hunter after my respects to you and family I seat myself to inform you of the condition of Mr. Hunter he is at this hospitle wounded and is compeled to dy there is no chance for him to recover his wound has mortified and I don't think he can live 24 hours long an I shal take care of him as long as he lives and shal right to you again and let you know how he dos Rebecca while I was riting he breathed his las breath I talked with him before he died he said he was ready to meet his heavenly Creater and was willing to dy I don't you ever can move him for his leg mortified so very bad that I think that's his will posibly for it to be done so he died ward K first division so nothing at preasant only I remain your friend even till death
>
> J C Miller[6]

Before W. A. died he entrusted his personal effects to Dr. Griffin. Inside his pocketbook was $62.00 in Confederate and state currency. Dr. Griffin wrote Young informing him of the sad news about his beloved father. He opened the note by sadly stating, "I have the painful duty of conveying to you the death of your dear father who expired this morning." In the letter Dr. Griffin also inquired as to the destination of W. A.'s belongings.

> I want you to write me what disposition to make of it to send it to you or to send it to your mother if I meet with an opportunity. His clothing is in the hands of the baggage made subject to your control.

Dr. Griffin closed his letter addressed to Young by "expressing deepest sympathy with you in this bereavement with best wishes for your happiness and prosperity." [7]

Proving himself a dutiful neighbor, Dr. Griffin accompanied the body to Oakwood Cemetery to mark the ground where W. A. would be laid to rest. The Confederate dead were being interred in Division G. A fresh trench, approximately one hundred feet long, designated Row G., awaited W. A.'s remains. These were carried along the trench to the first available space, where he was laid to rest in grave number 52. Dr. Griffin stood his distance watching as W. A. was covered with earth and a wooden marker with his number etched in was planted over the fresh grave. After the attendants moved down the line, Dr. Griffin approached the grave and marked the post with W. A.'s initials and the company and regiment he belonged to. Then Dr. Griffin returned to the hospital. [8]

Before Young could take his father's mantle upon himself, he needed to write to his mother concerning W. A.'s death. On August 27 he wrote:

> My Dearest Mother
> It is with sorrow that I write you these lines to inform you of the death of Pa He died on the 24inst at Richmond He was sent from Petersburg to Richmond on the 23 an died next morning at eight o clock The cause of his death was gangrean got into his wound
> Dr. T.C. Griffin was at the Hospital an wrote to me immediately an also to you T.C. Griffin attended his burial he marked his grave so that it could be identified if you should want his remains removed to Fla in the future I will send the letter with this that Dr. Griffin wrote to me.

For months W. A. had been praying his son would make peace with his Maker. Finally, with the painful passing of his father, Young confided to his mother where his faith must lie.

It greaves me but alas how soon may we follow The only consolation I can give you is to trust in him who made all things.

Realizing his mother's inability to fully manage the farming affairs Young instructed her to, "try an get Uncle James Young to take the business & his hand an manage it the best he knows how as to the best of his judgment." The weight of the entire, confused world seemed to be resting on Young's shoulders:

I must close hoping this may find you well this leaves me well give my love to all write soon.
Believe me as eaver Your affectionate son
Young [9]

Concerning W. A.'s personal effects, which included the pocketbook containing money, Young decided to forward it all to his mother. He felt she needed the money more than he did. First Lieutenant W. J. Barnett, of Company E, an acquaintance of the Hunters, had received a furlough and was returning to Florida. He agreed to carry W. A.'s belongings and pass them on to Rebecca. Barnett arrived in Lake City in early September; however, sickness prevented him from seeing Rebecca. On September 9, Barnett sent Rebecca a note:

Mrs. Hunter you have no doubt heard of the death of Mr Hunter he was wounded on the 21st and died on the 24th I have his pocket book and what money he had and would have been to see you before now but I have been confined to my bed ever since I have been at home as soon as I get able I will come and see you and tell you all I know about it he died hapy I write this to let you know the reason why I have not been to see you before now so I am yours [10]
Respectfully W. J. Barnett

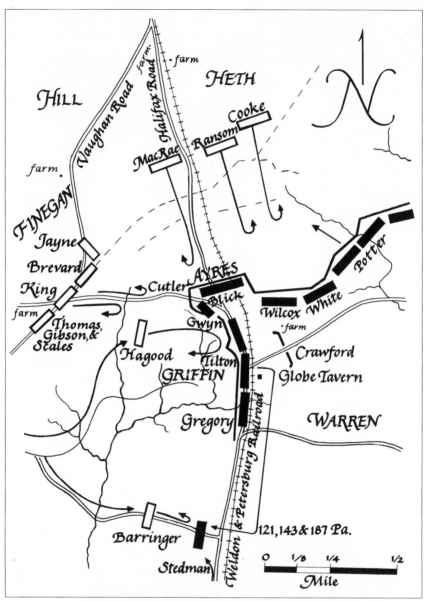

THE BATTLE OF GLOBE TAVERN, VIRGINIA
SUNDAY, AUGUST 21, 1864 — 10 A.M. POSITIONS

As an interesting side note, the records show two death dates for W. A. Hunter. The first, on August 24, from wounds received in battle, and second, on September 2, from "vulnus sclopeticum: Head." Vulnus sclopeticum was a generic medical term used widely by physicians during the Civil War. The Latin term was found on many records and simply means wound. In this case, inaccurately, wound to the head. Obviously, with all the extant first-hand documentation to support their claim, August 24 is the correct date. [11]

W. A. Hunter was forty-two years old.

9.

LET IT COME SOON OR LATE

Following their devastating loss at the Battle of Weldon Railroad, the Ninth Florida Regiment returned to their familiar trenches south of Petersburg. Young recorded on August 23, "One man a Mr. Grean deserted our Co. last night an went to the Yankees." Those who suffered through the continuing nightmare of death, sickness, filth, and starvation were the true heroes of the final months of the year as the Confederacy faltered and finally fell.[1]

Young Hunter, still an eighteen-year-old boy grieving over the loss of his father, admitted just how tired he was of the war in a letter to his mother.

You don't know how anxious I am to get home I want this cruel war to stop so that we all can get home and live in peace I have been in three fights since I have been in Va an you cant immagine how bad I feal when I hafto go in to a fight I have neaver went in one yet but what I thaught about you and all of my sisters and brothers you cant immagine what an awfull feeling it puts on any one to go down our Briggad has been in the trenches four weeaks last night for the last weeak it has been raining eavry day we have had a bad time the ditches about half full of mud an water we would get wett eavry day an night it rained but very liddle yesterday an has not rained any to day I hope it will quit for atime for this is one of the worst places when it is wett that I eaver saw[2]

Young Hunter had become a realist. The next morning he wrote:

Grant has a very hevy force around Petersberg I am a fraid we will have some hard fighting heare be fore long the Yankees have possession of the Weldon Supplies it would not surprise me if we would be into anouther fight with them ina few dayes.[3]

Young's prediction was correct. On August 24, Northern troops again threatened to destroy a section of the Weldon line. This time the force concentrated on Ream's Station, a short distance south of Globe Tavern. The Ninth Regiment, along with Mahone's division, marched down the road to Ream's Station and took part in an engagement to secure the lines from Federal threat. On this day, the men in faded gray were successful.[4]

August 24, 1864, the day W. A. Hunter died, was also the date of the final Hunter letter. Obviously, it was penned by Young.

The Yankees are in possession of the Weldon Road they are strongly fortified on the road an have a veary heavy force I think Grant has a veary heavy force around Petersberg at this time theire are a great many of our Brigade sick at this time it has rained a great deal for the last ten days this is one of the mudiest places that I eaver saw we have been in the trenches for four weeks I am tird of Virginia I want to get back to Fla. Whare I can get some milk butter potatoes syrup sugar an all of the good things that grow in Fla. I hear that East Fla. Is expected to be evacuated an given up to the Yanks I hope it is not so. Fla. Has as much right for protection as any oather state an I think she ought to have it she has done as much for the Confederacy according to her population as any oather state an their fore she ought to have protection

Dear Sister I hope East Fla. Will not be evacuated but if it is an the Yanks come through the county try an get out of theire reach if it is possible I think it a good idier to seand the cotton up to Madison try to save it if possible you wanted to know if I wanted woolen socks if you can see a chance send me one pair I have got two pair of cotton ones at present seand me a few poasttage stamps some time when you write Write soon give my love to all[5]

Believe me as eaver your Brother

Young Hunter

With the last of the Hunter letters, the personal history of the Ninth Regiment ends abruptly.

However the documented military history continued. From September until the end of 1864, Young and his regiment were involved in three engagements. Fort Harrison, a strategic Confederate garrison protecting the southeastern corner of Richmond line, became the target of Federal attack in late September. The battle began and soon the Confederate fort succumbed to the superior numbers of the Federal army. Then, on September 30, a Confederate force including the Ninth Regiment marched north of the Appomattox and James Rivers and attacked the Federals at Fort Harrison in an attempt to dislodge the enemy. The expedition was unsuccessful and the Confederate force returned to the Petersburg trenches.[6]

October followed with a victory on the 27th at Burgess' Mill located on Hatcher's Run, west of Boydton Plank Road. The enemy was attempting to capture Petersburg by skirting the city in a flanking maneuver. The Ninth Regiment was pulled out of a quiet sector of trench located between the Appomattox River and Battery Number 45 and rushed to Burgess's Mill. Mahone's division charged the enemy and drove them back, capturing four-hundred prisoners, three stands of colors, and six artillery pieces.[7]

As winter approached, the Ninth Regiment concentrated its efforts on building huts for winter quarters. The regiment was in reserve near Fort Gregg, south of Petersburg, and suffered considerably for the want of proper winter clothing. However, enemy action was light, and the front remained quiet.[8]

In early December a Federal force advanced on Petersburg from the south. It was believed their objective was to destroy the vital bridge spanning the Roanoke River. Wade Hampton's cavalry was immediately dispatched to intercept and harass the Union troops until a Confederate infantry force, including the Ninth Regiment, could arrive. The Ninth Regiment was pulled from the trenches near Petersburg and forced to march fifty miles, over frozen, bleak roads, to Hicksford or Belfield, Virginia on the Meherrin River. When the Confederates reached Belfield, they were ordered to charge and destroy the Federal force numbering 20,000 men. Inclement winter weather conditions combined with fatigue from the long march caused the Southern force to move slowly, giving the Union force time to fall back. After the Federal retreat, the Ninth Regiment returned to its Petersburg trenches footsore and hobbling painfully through snow and ice.[9]

At this time regimental morale was probably at its lowest since the men had arrived in Virginia. As noted historian, Clement Eaton, stated in his monumental work, *The Southern Confederacy,* the South "lost the will to fight." The men lost hope of victory. When Abraham Lincoln was re-elected, Southern morale plummeted further as the Father of Emancipation was granted four more years in office. Knowing the war was lost, and unwilling to endure the common depravations of the Confederate army during the winter of 1864, as has been said, more Floridians in Finegan's brigade deserted to Union lines.

Stanhope Harris, a close friend of the Hunter family and one of the many neighbors who emigrated from Newberry County, South Carolina, left at this time. Harris escaped to Union lines, surrendered, and was sent to City Point where he then swore the oath of allegiance to the United States. From City Point, he was sent to Washington D. C. for a short time, then moved on to Philadelphia where he spent the duration of the war. Over half the Floridian deserters were processed in this manner.[10] These deserters paid a high price—they were labeled traitors. Obviously they were dishonored and they returned to family and property in Florida to suffer ridicule, physical and mental harassment and ostracism. The Hunters had chosen a higher way.

In January 1865 a large and influential portion of the Confederate senators from Florida, "in compliance with the constituents," requested that General Finegan be transferred to Florida. The troops sensed the despondency of their commander. Senators Baker and Maxwell submitted their request to President Davis. Finegan's commanding officer, General Mahone, was absent, so on January 23, 1865, Finegan wrote the Assistant Adjutant General, Colonel Walter H. Taylor requesting the transfer be suspended until General Mahone returned to active duty.

Finegan trusted Mahone to choose a reasonable man among the Florida ranks to lead his brigade. He ended his letter explaining why he desired to return to Florida:

> I am between fifty-four and fifty-five years of age, and have been in the State and Confederate service about four years, and have not in that time been absent one week from duty. While this application has not been made at my solicitation, it would be agreeable to me if I could be transferred to a climate more con-

genial to my health and age, and where my intimate knowledge of the country and people would enable me to render more service than I possibly can do in command of a small brigade.[11]

Two months passed before Finegan's request would be granted, but on March 20, 1865, the general who had led his men to glory at Olustee and Cold Harbor was reassigned to Florida.[12]

The final blow to morale occurred in early April when news of Governor Milton's death reached the Florida troops in Virginia. Milton had been a colorful leader throughout the war, a champion of soldiers and Florida's individual rights. As the conflict wound down, he vehemently proclaimed his state was nearly "a waste." He exhorted all Floridians to sacrifice all to gain independence. In his final appearance before the Florida legislature he admitted, "Death would be preferable to Union." On April 1, just eight days before Lee's surrender, a despondent Milton returned to his plantation. While his daughter prepared his "homecoming" meal, the governor retired to his chambers and fired a shotgun blast into his head.[13]

The Ninth saw action on February 6, near Hatcher's Run, as the Federals attempted to extend their line of battle and raid Lee's wagon trains. The battle being waged on General John Gordon's front repelled the enemy, but a second assault drove Rebel lines back until Finegan rushed his regiments in, driving out the enemy. The Ninth Regiment kept in close pursuit of its enemy, taking pot shots when the opportunity allowed. However, as dusk shrouded the evening sky, the fight broke off, affording the Federal force an opportunity to dig in, and succeed in its goal of extending the front lines. The Battle of Hatcher's Run proved to be a moral victory for the Confederacy, delaying the raids upon Lee's supply lines. Hatcher's Run was General Finegan's late, shining hour: he commanded four brigades and successfully stayed the advance of four Union divisions.[14]

In late February rumors concerning troop movements abounded in the ranks of the Ninth Regiment. It was generally felt that Mahone's division would be sent south toward North Carolina or move north of the Appomattox River. Rumors became reality in March when the division moved to occupy the Howlett line across the neck of the Bermuda Hundred, north of the Appomattox River, relieving General Pickett. Mahone had kept his division a solid, battle-ready fighting force, and for this reason he was entrusted with guarding the Howlett line. Life was quiet along the Howlett line until the morning of April 2 when Union forces skirmished with Mahone's division. Later that same day, General Lee's lines south of Petersburg crumbled and dissolved, as the journey toward the end commenced.[15]

General Lee sent a dispatch to Mahone ordering him to remove to Amelia Courthouse, thirty-nine miles away. Mahone's division left their trenches the night of April 2. In actuality, the division began its retreat early in the morning of the third when Mahone guided his men to Chesterfield Courthouse, then to Goode's Bridge.[16]

Near Goode's Bridge the road coming down from Richmond intersected with the road taken by Mahone's force. It was the task of Mahone to hold the bridge securely until General Richard Ewell's force from Richmond arrived and crossed the bridge. At Goode's Bridge the division waited anxiously until the fourth when they again commenced the retreat to Amelia Courthouse.[17]

Retreating was a difficult task, as the country roads were strewn with debris and the roadway crowded with an endless stream of refugee women with children fleeing Petersburg. When the regiment reached Chester, the sun was rising on the morning of the third, still not visible through the puffy gray clouds. The soldiers' attention was diverted when a "terrific" explosion rocked the earth behind them. As the men turned their attention backward, they realized the magazine at Drewry's Bluff had been destroyed and as Mahone stated, ". . . lighted the heavens and fairly shook the earth in all that region."[18]

Mahone's division reached Amelia Courthouse in the early morning hours of Wednesday, April 5. It was here the Floridians and all of Mahone's division learned of the tragic death of General A. P. Hill, their corps commander, on April 2. Shortly after one o'clock on the fifth, Mahone's force left the courthouse. The day was cloudy and drizzle fell on the retreating party. The Ninth Regiment fell back along the road heading to Jetersville near the Burkeville Railroad line, following Rooney Lee's cavalry.[19]

In the early morning hours of April 6, Mahone's division stopped at Saylor's Creek, a tributary of the Appomattox River, to eat their breakfast. General Richard Anderson's force was behind Mahone's and was being threatened by Federal troops. General Lee ordered Mahone to dispatch a brigade to Anderson's aid. Mahone ordered the Florida brigade, now under the command of Colonel David Lang of the Eighth Regiment, down the road to assist Anderson. Only three of the six Florida regiments parted from the main force, the Fifth, Eighth, and Eleventh Regiments, the latter commanded by Colonel Theodore W. Brevard. The remainder of the Florida brigade retired, along with the main body of Mahone's division, to a nearby hilltop and watched helplessly, agonizingly, as their friends, relatives, and fellow statesmen were swiftly and efficiently captured by Colonel George Custer's Union cavalry. It was a decisive blow to Finegan's brigade. Looking on sadly, the soldiers mused that the end had to be near.[20]

Following its loss at Saylor's Creek the Southern army made haste to put the Appomattox River between the enemy and itself. The night of April 6, the Ninth Regiment crossed High Bridge spanning the Appomattox. General Lee left orders with Mahone to burn the vital bridge once all Confederates had crossed. Mahone was forced to delay the burning of the bridge until General Gordon's Second Corps reached it. During this delay, Mahone took the opportunity to reconnoiter the area for a passable road to Farmville. Before departing, he left orders with a Colonel Tallcott to inform Gordon that he must burn the bridge once his force had crossed. Mahone spent the balance of the night exploring local roads and when he returned at dawn of the seventh, he saw the enemy converging on the unburned bridge. Quickly Mahone ordered the bridge destroyed by fire. Although the bridge was put to the torch, the Federal force fell upon it quickly and extinguished the flames in short order. Lee and other corps commanders later blamed Mahone for the debacle of High Bridge, since he could not be found to dispatch the order to burn the bridge.[21]

Soon the enemy continued to press upon the retreating Confederate army that was now making for Lynchburg. Later the same day, the Ninth Florida Regiment reached Farmville, stopping to form a battle line and commenced to fight its last battle of the war. The enemy was pressing close to the Ninth's rear. Mahone stopped his division to skirmish with the enemy in order to widen the distance between the Federals and Lee's army. The engagement started as picket skirmishing. Soon the Federals attacked, but were easily repelled. The Union forces reformed, massing their forces in a ravine on the Confederate's left. Noticing this movement, the Ninth took part in an assault that broke Federal strategy and resulted in the capture of 1,100 Union prisoners.[22]

The Battle of Farmville gave Lee a little more time to extend the doomed Confederate flight to North Carolina. However, victory was short-lived—surrounded on April 9, 1865, Lee surrendered to General Grant at Appomattox Courthouse.

On April 12 the formal surrender commenced. The Ninth Regiment, one of the last regiments in surrender line, paraded up from the creek bottom where it camped, to the top of the hill. It followed General Wilcox's men into surrender triangle, relinquishing all muskets, sidearms, bayonets, and regimental flags. Standing like a "stone wall" and breaking ranks only when ordered to by Mahone or Lee, the regiment received its parole passes and marched away from Appomattox, heading for home.

Officially, the Ninth Florida Regiment had been in existence less than one year; however, many of the men had been fighting for the Confederacy since early 1862. They fought a heated battle at Olustee to save their home state and were heroes at the Battle of Cold Harbor. They suffered from disease, want of food and proper clothing, merciless marches, taxing work details, the effects of the harsh climate and countless other hardships. On the records, 1,292 men enrolled in the Ninth Regiment but a mere 109 were present to surrender at Appomattox.[23]

Sometime between his father's death and the surrender, Young Hunter was promoted to corporal. He survived the conflict, and was paroled at Appomattox. Young Hunter was typical of the faithful few who honored the state and the Confederacy by staying at their posts through some of the most mentally, physically and spiritually debilitating circumstances nineteenth century man could devise. He returned to his family in Florida where he managed his father's farm.

AFTERWORD

After receiving his parole pass at Appomattox Courthouse, Young began his long and arduous journey home. No letters or documents remain explaining how he returned home. Possibly he walked the six hundred miles back to Florida.

He was home. The nightmare which had lasted fifteen months was finally over. Young began a new life with new responsibilities. He managed his father's farm with a new form of labor. Young successfully directed the business affairs through the new era showing profits along the way. He became the man of the family—W. A. would have been proud.

As with most Southern families, the war exacted a costly toll upon the extended Hunter family. W. A.'s brother-in-law Joseph Young had died a slow, agonizing death after receiving a mortal wound during the Battle of Olustee in 1864. He left behind a young wife, Arietta, and their infant daughter, Alma.

W. A.'s brother John C. did not escape unscathed—his son Nathan died after receiving a mortal wound in the early stages of the Olustee campaign. John C. himself contracted a cold while retrieving Nathan's body in February 1864 and died as a result of pneumonia the following June. John C.'s oldest son, Thompson Hunter, died in a Corinth, Mississippi, hospital only days before Lee's surrender in Virginia. Finally, W. A.'s passing completed the lamentable tragedy that the Hunter family had suffered as a result of the destructive conflict.

Florida did not seem to be much different from swampy Virginia in terms of life expectancy. In 1868 at age twenty, Young's sister Susannah died. Belle followed her older sister in death in 1875 at the age of seventeen, dying of diphtheria. On June 9, 1870, Young's beloved mother, Rebecca Caroline, passed away. W. A.'s bride was forty-six when she died.

Shortly upon his return from Virginia, Young married a woman named Elmira Roberts. When she died, Young remarried; this time his bride was his Aunt Arietta. Arietta bore Young five children: Lena,

Josephus, Nellie, Hoyt and Young, of whom only the latter lived past the age of four. The household of Young's sister Melissa was also one of sorrow, as seven of her nine children died in childhood. Young's little sister Estelle suffered the same fate, with four of her five children expiring before reaching four years of age.

The Hunter letters might possibly have slipped into oblivion if not for the bold actions taken by Estelle. Estelle's first husband, Joel Niblack, died as a young man in 1886. Estelle later remarried Mr. Frank Puckett. Estelle had grown eccentric and the two found they could not live together any longer. So divorcing Puckett, Estelle packed her belongings, along with the war letters of W. A. and Young, and moved with her son Thompson to Fort Myers. There she treasured the letters. Her son kept the letters following Estelle's death in 1937, storing them in the hot and humid attic of the house he had built on the corner of Broadway and Edison.

Young's brother Hayne also suffered an ill-fated history. He grew up a rough, quarrelsome man who carried a large hunting knife on his hip at all times. In 1914, a Mr. Will Cook tarnished the honor of Hayne's daughter, forcing Hayne to avenge her fallen dignity. Hayne met Will Cook on the streets of Lake City with a 22-gauge rifle in his hands, facing Cook's own shotgun. Hayne fired first and hit Cook in the chest forcing him to the ground. Cook, still grasping his gun, aimed from the dirt and fired at Hayne. The full charge hit Hayne in the abdomen. Both men were carried to a nearby saloon and laid out upon pool tables. Will Cook survived the shooting, but Hayne's wound proved mortal. Before slipping away, he repented of his evil ways and asked Mr. Cook's forgiveness.

What of Young Hunter, the boy who "enjoyed" himself initially, but later itched to get home? His life also ended prematurely. The Columbia County Courthouse, along with all records, burned to the ground. All that is known is that William Young Hunter, veteran of the worst war in American history, died on Thursday, September 3, 1874. He was twenty-eight.

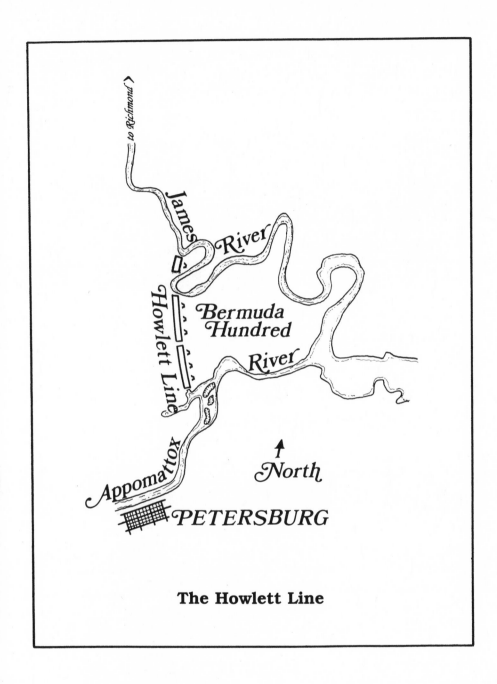

The Howlett Line

Florida State Archives

Governor John Milton, Florida's Civil War governor, called one of the "Maverick" Southern governors, committed suicide one week before Appomattox.

Governor Abraham Allison was head of Florida's government for just two weeks in 1865.

Captain J. J. Dickison, cavalry officer who turned back Federal expedition at Gainesville in 1864.

Florida State Archives

NOTES

Chapter Two

1. Charleton W. Tebeau, *A History of Florida* (Coral Gables: University of Miami Press, 1971), p. 199; Official Records of the Armies (ORA), series 4, vol. 2, p. 648.
2. Fred L. Robertson, *Soldiers of Florida in the Seminole, Indian, Civil, and Spanish-American Wars* (Live Oak, 1903), p. 35.
3. Ibid., p. 36.
4. J. J. Dickison, *Confederate Military History: Florida* (Atlanta, 1899), vol. 11, p. 27; Robertson, p. 38.
5. Dickison, *Confederate Military History*, vol. 11, pp. 28-30; Robertson, p. 39.
6. Samuel Proctor, ed. *Florida a Hundred Years Ago* (Tallahassee, 1963), October 1863; Karl H. Grismer, *The Story of Fort Myers* (Fort Myers Beach, 1982), p. 78; ORA, series 1, vol. 23, part 2, p. 702; Robert A. Taylor, *Rebel Storehouse: Florida in the Confederate Economy* (Tuscaloosa, 1995), pp. 98, 126.
7. Ed Gleeson, *Erin Go Gray* (Carmel, Indiana, 1997), p. 3.
8. Ibid., p. 4.
9. Ibid.
10. Ibid., pp. 4-6.
11. Robertson, pp. 38-40, 77, 99-102, 118-119.
12. Ibid., pp. 135, 153, 170, 186.
13. National Archives Washington, D. C., Compiled Military Service Records (MSR) of the Ninth Florida Regiment, Records Group 109, reels 87-92; ORA, series 2, vol. 4, p. 249.
14. Florida State Library, Tallahassee, Florida. Confederate pension records of Asa A. Stewart; United States Census of 1860, Columbia County Agricultural Schedule, Yonge Library, University of Florida; Census, Slave Schedule; MSR, Company E.
15. MSR, Company E.
16. Ibid.
17. MSR, W. A. Hunter.

18. Proctor, August 1861; Civil War letters of William Addison Hunter (W. A. Hunter) written to Rebecca Hunter, February 9, 1864, in possession of the author; ORA, series 1, vol. 28, p. 328.
19. ORA, series 1, vol. 14, pp. 227, 229, 850.
20. MSR, Company E.
21. MSR, Company E; Susan E. Burdett, "The Military Career of Brigadier General Joseph Finegan of Florida," (Masters Thesis, Columbia University, 1930), p. 3.
22. MSR, Company E; W. A. Hunter letter to Rebecca Hunter, February 9, 1864.
23. MSR, Ninth Florida Regiment.
24. Ibid.
25. MSR, William Young Hunter (Young Hunter).

Chapter Three

1. MSR, John M. Martin.
2. "Last Roll," *Confederate Veteran Magazine*, (December 1918), vol. 25, p. 507; Dickison, *Confederate Military History*, vol. 11, pp. 317-318.
3. MSR, Company B.
4. ORA, series 1, vol. 53, pp. 224-225, 233-234.
5. Ibid., pp. 233-234; MSR, John W. Pearson.
6. ORA, series 1, vol. 14, pp. 111-112.
7. MSR, Company B.
8. Ibid.
9. MSR, Company D.
10. Ibid.
11. MSR, Company D, John and Joseph Bryan; MSR, James F. Tucker.
12. MSR, Company D, Joseph A. Young.
13. ORA, series 1, vol. 28, p. 413.
14. ORA, series 1, vol. 53, pp. 233-234.
15. ORA, series 1, vol. 28, p. 402; John E. Johns, *Florida During the Civil War* (Gainesville, 1963), p. 161.
16. Johns, p. 160.
17. Ibid., p. 162.
18. Johns, pp. 162-163; ORA, series 1, vol. 28, pp. 401-403.

19. ORA, series 1, vol. 28, pp. 402-403.

20. Ibid., p. 402.

21. Johns, pp. 161-162.

22. ORA, series 1, vol. 35, pp. 485-486.

23. ORA, series 1, vol. 28, pp. 413, 469; part 2, p. 567.

24. Ibid., vol. 28, pp. 440, 577, 592.

Chapter Four

1. MSR, Asa A. Stewart; MSR, Green H. Hunter; *The New York Times*, February 20, 1864; David J. Coles, "A Fight, A Licking, and a Footrace: The 1864 Florida Campaign and the Battle of Olustee," (Masters Thesis, Florida State University, 1985), pp. 43-46; MSR, Joseph Barco; MSR, Jacob Eichelberger.

2. W. A. Hunter, February 9, 1864.

3. Civil War letters of William Young Hunter (Young Hunter) written to Rebecca and Melissa Hunter, February 10, 1864, in possession of the author.

4. Ibid.

5. Ibid.

6. *The New York Times*, February 20, 1864.

7. *The Baker County Press*, August 26, 1976, p. 2.

8. Civil War letters of Joseph A. Young (Joseph Young), February 13, 1864, Senseman private collection, Fort Myers; *The Baker County Press*, August 26, 1976, p. 2.

9. *The Baker County Press*, August 26, 1976, p. 2.

10. W. A. Hunter, undated, but events described within the letter suggest draft date as February 11, 1864.

11. Ibid.

12. Coles, pp. 49, 68; *Charleston Daily Courier*, February 12, 1864; Joseph Young, February 13, 1864.

13. Joseph Young, February 18, 1864.

14. *The New York Times*, February 20, 1864; Johns, p. 197.

15. ORA, series 1, vol. 35, part 1, p. 331; Coles, p. 110.

16. Dickison, *Confederate Military History*, vol. 11, pp. 61-62.

17. ORA, series 1, vol. 35, part 1, p. 344.

18. Ibid.
19. Dickison, *Confederate Military History*, vol. 11, p. 72.
20. ORA, series 1, vol. 35, part 1, p. 332; Gleeson, pp. 17-18.
21. Gleeson, p. 18.
22. Tebeau, p. 215; MSR, Ninth Florida Regiment.
23. MSR, Thomas Griffin; MSR, Joseph A. Young.
24. *Charleston Daily Courier*, February 24, 1864.
25. Dickison, *Confederate Military History*, vol. 11, p. 81; ORA, series 1, vol. 14, pp. 850-851.
26. Young Hunter, March 14, 1864; W. A. Hunter, May 3, 1864.
27. W. A. Hunter, March 22, 1864.
28. W. A. Hunter, April 20, 1864.
29. W. A. Hunter, March 22, 1864.
30. W. A. Hunter, April 20, 1864.
31. W. A. Hunter, May 3, 1864.
32. W. A. Hunter, April 20, 1864.
33. MSR, Ninth Florida Regiment. Each record card shows date of organization.
34. ORA, series 1, vol. 35, part 2, pp. 485, 488, 492.
35. W. A. Hunter, May 20, 1864.
36. Ibid.
37. MSR, Ninth Florida Regiment. The ORA maintains only 425 men belonging to the regiment actually made the trip north, but the military service records of the regiment reveal 656 men made the trip.
38. W. A. Hunter, May 20, 1864.
39. Ibid.
40. Ibid.
41. Ibid.
42. ORA, series 1, vol. 51, part 2, p. 956; W. A. Hunter, May 22, 1864.
43. W. A. Hunter, May 22, 1864.
44. Ibid.
45. ORA, series 1, vol. 36, part 2, p. 825; W. A. Hunter, May 25, 1864.
46. W. A. Hunter, May 25, 1864.
47. ORA, series 1, vol. 36, part 3, p. 832.

Chapter Five

1. W. A. Hunter, May 26, 1864.
2. W. A. Hunter, May 26, 1864; Robertson, p. 206; Nelson Morehouse Blake, *William Mahone of Virginia: Soldier and Political Insurgent* (Richmond, 1935), p. 49.
3. W. A. Hunter, May 26, 1864.
4. Ibid.
5. W. A. Hunter, May 29, 1864; Robertson, p. 335; Proctor, June 1864; ORA, series 1, vol. 36, part 3, p. 843; W. A. Hunter, May 29, 1864.
6. Douglas Southall Freeman, *R. E. Lee* (New York, 1937), vol. 3, p. 364.
7. W. A. Hunter, May 29, 1864.
8. Ibid.
9. W. A. Hunter, May 31, 1864.
10. Ibid.
11. ORA, series 1, vol. 36, part 1, pp. 1031-1032; Blake, p. 50.
12. James H. Lane, "History of Lane's North Carolina Brigade," *Southern Historical Society Papers* (Richmond), vol. 9, p. 244; Freeman, *R. E. Lee*, vol. 3, pp. 381-383; ORA, series 1, vol. 36, part 1, p. 662; MSR, Charles Anderson; MSR, William H. Allen.
13. Freeman, *R. E. Lee*, vol. 3, p. 383.
14. Burdett, p. 15; ORA, series 1, vol. 36, part 2, p. 1013; part 3, pp. 836, 843.
15. ORA, series 1, vol. 36, part 2, p. 1013; part 3, pp. 836, 843.
16. ORA, series 1, vol. 51, part 2, pp. 982-983.
17. Robertson, p. 329; Francis P. Fleming, *The Florida Troops in Virginia* (Jacksonville, 1884), p. 99.
18. Gleeson, p. 25.
19. W. A. Hunter, June 5, 1864.
20. Ibid.
21. MSR, Ninth Florida Regiment; MSR, James Wimberly.
22. MSR, Pickens B. Bird; *Register of Confederate Dead Interred in Hollywood Cemetery, Richmond, Virginia* (Richmond, 1969).
23. MSR, James O. Owens; MSR, Benjamin L. Reynolds; MSR, Benjamin B. Lane.
24. MSR, Robert D. Harrison.

25. *Roll of Honour* (CMLS), vol. 313, no. 160; MSR, James F. Tucker.

26. E. P. Alexander, *Military Memoirs of a Confederate* (New York, 1907), p. 542; General Andrew A. Humphreys, *Humphreys' Campaigns* (New York, 1883), p. 193.

27. Bertram H. Groene, ed., "Civil War Letters of David Lang," *Florida Historical Quarterly* (FHQ), vol. 54 (January 1976), pp. 363-364.

28. Young Hunter, June 16, 1864.

29. W. A. Hunter, June 16, 1864; Young Hunter, June 16, 1864.

30. W. A. Hunter, June 16, 1864.

31. Ibid.

32. W. A. Hunter, June 17, 1864.

33. Douglas Southall Freeman, *Lee's Lieutenants: A Study in Command* (New York, 1951), vol. 3, pp. 537, 553.

34. W. A. Hunter, June 19, 1864.

35. W. A. Hunter, June 20, 1864.

36. W. A. Hunter, June 19, 1864.

37. W. A. Hunter, June 16, 1864; Young Hunter, June 16, 1864.

38. W. A. Hunter, June 20, 1864.

39. W. A. Hunter, June 17, 1864.

40. Freeman, *Lee's Lieutenants*, vol. 3, pp. 537-539, Finegan's troops were mainly credited for this victory; Freeman, *R. E. Lee*, vol. 3, p. 453; ORA, series 1, vol. 40, part 2, p. 375.

41. ORA, series 1, vol. 40, part 1, pp. 629-630.

42. MSR, W. P. Roberts; MSR, David L. White.

43. MSR, Charles M. Brown; MSR, John W. Marston.

44. MSR, Robert G. McEwen; MSR, James R. Williams.

45. W. A. Hunter, June 28, 1864.

Chapter Six

1. MSR, Ninth Florida Regiment; Freeman, *R. E. Lee*, vol. 3, pp. 496-497.

2. W. A. Hunter, June 16, 1864; June 17, 1864; July 19, 1864; August 5, 1864; MSR, Ninth Florida Regiment.

3. W. A. Hunter, June 27, 1864; Young Hunter, June 27, 1864.

4. W. A. Hunter, July 17, 1864; July 27, 1864.

5. W. A. Hunter, July 17, 1864.

6. Theresa Yaeger Palmer, *The Palmer Physicians*, (manuscript in Yonge Library, Gainesville, Florida), n/p.; W. A. Hunter, July 27, 1864.

7. ORA, series 1, vol. 40, part 3, pp. 1188-1189.

8. Proctor, December 1864, p. 2. This is a classic example of what Dr. Frank Owsley describes in his book, *States Rights In the Confederacy*: that mustang Confederate governors always sought to work in opposition to the objectives of the central government.

9. MSR, Ninth Florida Regiment.

10. W. A. Hunter, June 16, 1864; Groene, p. 365; W. A. Hunter, July 19, 1864; July 17, 1864.

11. W. A. Hunter, July 27, 1864.

12. Young Hunter, August 22, 1864.

13. W. A. Hunter, July 27, 1864.

14. Young Hunter, June 16, 1864.

15. ORA, series 1, vol. 40, part 3, p. 127; W. A. Hunter, July 9, 1864.

16. W. A. Hunter, July 9, 1864; August 15, 1864.

17. MSR, John M. Martin; MSR, Company B.

18. ORA, series 1, vol. 46, part 2, p. 1145.

19. Ibid., p. 1146.

20. W. A. Hunter, August 15, 1864; Young Hunter, July 24, 1864.

21. W. A. Hunter, July 1864, exact date unknown; July 27, 1864. A quire contains 24 sheets of paper.

22. ORA, series 1, vol. 46, part 2, p. 1145.

23. W. A. Hunter, June 19, 1864.

24. W. A. Hunter, June 25, 1864.

25. W. A. Hunter, June 27, 1864.

26. W. A. Hunter, August 14, 1864.

27. W. A. Hunter, July 17, 1864.

28. W. A. Hunter, July 10, 1864; July 14, 1864.

29. W. A. Hunter, July 27, 1864; August 5, 1864.

30. W. A. Hunter, July 9, 1864.

31. W. A. Hunter, July 3, 1864.

32. W. A. Hunter, June 27, 1864; July 1864; June 16, 1864.

33. W. A. Hunter, July 10, 1864; August 15, 1864.

34. Young Hunter, August 22, 1864.

35. W. A. Hunter, June 16, 1864; Young Hunter, July 24, 1864.

36. W. A. Hunter, July 26, 1864.

37. W. A. Hunter, July 4, 1864; June 25, 1864; July 21, 1864.

38. W. A. Hunter, July 19, 1864.

39. W. A. Hunter, July 21, 1864; August 4, 1864.

40. W. A. Hunter, June 5, 1864.

41. W. A. Hunter, August 15, 1864.

42. Young Hunter, July 24, 1864.

43. MSR, Samuel Worthington; Thomas Winn, Milton's aide-de-camp letter found in Winn's file.

44. Douglas Southall Freeman, *A Calendar of Confederate Papers* (Richmond, 1908), p. 276.

45. W. A. Hunter, July 9, 1864.

46. W. A. Hunter, July 17, 1864; Groene, p. 365.

47. Proctor, August 1861, p. 1; Young Hunter, July 24, 1864; W. A. Hunter, July 27, 1864.

48. W. A. Hunter, June 5, 1864; July 14, 1864.

49. W. A. Hunter, July 27, 1864; July 10, 1864.

50. Young Hunter, July 24, 1864.

51. Young Hunter, August 24, 1864.

52. W. A. Hunter, August 14, 1864.

53. MSR, John M. Martin; Robertson, p. 208.

54. W. A. Hunter, July 17, 1864; July 27, 1864.

55. National Archives, Washington, D. C., Inspection Reports of Finegan's Brigade, Records Group 109, February 25, 1865; Inspection Reports, September 30, 1864; Inspection Reports, December 30, 1864.

56. MSR, Ninth Florida Regiment.

57. MSR, Isaac J. Wiley; MSR, Isham Cooper, Tenth Florida Regiment.

58. MSR, Ninth Florida Regiment.

59. ORA, series 1, vol. 40, part 3, p. 226; vol. 46, part 2, p. 688.

60. ORA, series 1, vol. 40, part 3, p. 209; vol. 42, part 3, p. 1249; vol. 46, part 2, p. 1148.

61. Gilbert Adams Hays, *Under the Red Patch* (Pittsburgh, 1908), p. 271.

62. Young Hunter, August 24, 1864.

63. MSR, Ninth Florida Regiment.

Chapter Seven

1. Young Hunter, July 24, 1864; W. A. Hunter, July 27, 1864.
2. Blake, p. 54.
3. Gary Loderhose, "The Battle of the Crater," *The Drummer's Roll: A Journal of Florida Soldiers During the Civil War*, vol. 1, issue 2 (April 1998), p. 4.
4. Blake, p. 54.
5. Freeman, *R. E. Lee*, vol. 3, p. 467; W. A. Hunter, July 31, 1864.
6. ORA, series 1, vol. 36, part 1, p. 27.
7. W. A. Hunter, July 31, 1864.
8. W. A. Hunter, August 1, 1864.
9. W. A. Hunter, August 5, 1864.
10. W. A. Hunter, August 15, 1864.
11. W. A. Hunter, August 3, 1864.
12. W. A. Hunter, August 4, 1864.
13. W. A. Hunter, August 5, 1864.
14. W. A. Hunter, August 14, 1864.
15. W. A. Hunter, August 15, 1864.
16. W. A. Hunter, August 14, 1864.
17. Freeman, *Lee's Lieutenants*, vol. 3, pp. 588-589; ORA, series 1, vol. 42, part 1, pp. 936, 939; part 2, p. 1195.
18. Freeman, *Lee's Lieutenants*, vol. 3, pp. 588-589; *R. E. Lee*, vol. 3, p. 487; Young Hunter, August 22, 1864.
19. Proctor, September 1864, p. 1; Robertson, p. 209; MSR, John W. Pearson; *Richmond Daily Examiner*, August 25, 1864.
20. Letter of an unidentified soldier belonging to Finegan's brigade, in possession of the author, August 22, 1864.

Chapter Eight

1. Young Hunter, August 22, 1864.
2. Young Hunter, August 24, 1864.
3. MSR, W. A. Hunter.
4. Civil War letter of T. C. Griffin, August 24, 1864, Senseman private collection, Fort Myers.
5. Ibid.

6. Civil War letter of Jacob C. Miller, August 24, 1864, Senseman private collection, Fort Myers.
7. Griffin, August 24, 1864.
8. Ibid.
9. Young Hunter, August 27, 1864.
10. Civil War letter of W. J. Barnett, September 9, 1864, Senseman private collection, Fort Myers.
11. MSR, W. A. Hunter.

Chapter Nine

1. Young Hunter, August 23, 1864.
2. Young Hunter, August 22, 1864.
3. Young Hunter, August 23, 1864.
4. Freeman, *Lee's Lieutenants*, vol. 3, p. 589.
5. Young Hunter, August 24, 1864. This is the last letter in possession of the author. Young's letter dated August 27, 1864, part of the Senseman collection, is the last surviving Civil War letter written by Young Hunter.
6. Freeman, *Lee's Lieutenants*, vol. 3, p. 592; ORA, series 1, vol. 42, part 3, pp. 80-81.
7. Freeman, *Lee's Lieutenants*, vol. 3, p. 615; *R. E. Lee*, vol. 3, p. 514; Blake, p. 61.
8. ORA, vol. 42, part 3, pp. 610-613.
9. Freeman, *Lee's Lieutenants*, vol. 3, p. 616; ORA, series 1, vol. 42, part 1, p. 951; Dickison, vol. 11, p. 159; Proctor, December 1864, p. 3; Robertson, p. 207.
10. MSR, Stanhope Harris.
11. ORA, series 1, vol. 46, part 2, p. 1128.
12. Ibid., part 3, p. 1327.
13. Gene M. Burnett, *Florida's Past: People and Events That Shaped the State* (Englewood, 1986), vol. 1, pp. 197-200; Proctor, April, 1865, p. 1.
14. *Richmond Whig*, February 8, 1865; Blake, p. 63; Gleeson, pp. 34-40.
15. ORA, series 1, vol. 46, part 2, pp. 659-662; Blake, p. 63; Freeman, *Lee's Lieutenants*, vol. 3, p. 675; ORA, series 1, vol. 46, part 3, p. 441.

16. William Mahone, "On the Road to Appomattox", *Civil War Times Illustrated* vol. 9 (January 9, 1970), p. 7.
17. Mahone, p. 8; Freeman, *Lee's Lieutenants*, vol. 3, pp. 690-691.
18. Mahone, p. 7.
19. Mahone, p. 8; Freeman, *Lee's Lieutenants*, vol. 3, p. 692.
20. ORA, series 1, vol. 46, part 1. pp. 1265, 1294; Mahone, p. 9; Proctor, April 1865, p. 2; Confederate Military History, vol. 11, p. 160; Freeman, *Lee's Lieutenants*; vol. 3, p. 710.
21. Freeman, *Lee's Lieutenants*, vol. 3, pp. 712-714; Mahone, p. 42.
22. Freeman, *Lee's Lieutenants*, vol. 3, p. 716; Confederate Military History, vol.11, p. 160.
23. ORA, series 1, vol. 46, part 3, p. 706; Blake, p. 65; MSR, Ninth Florida Regiment; "Paroles of the Army of Northern Virginia," *Southern Historical Society Papers*, vol. 15, pp. 309-310.

Index